"Jackson Bliss, human kaleidoscope  plays with, and creates characters with aliveness. This writer's insatia we do in it transforms into gorgeous sentences and playful/serious inquiry here. *Counterfactual Love Stories* is a book of inspiring vitality and perception."

—**AIMEE BENDER**, author of *The Butterfly Lampshade*

"Of course the cover color of Jackson Bliss's epochal collection for the anthropocene, *Counterfactual Love Stories & Other Experiments*, is fetching Coral. This book is made up of storied and honeycombed restless ramparts and multi-chambered reefs of intricate interlocking organic masonry, both delicate and enduring. Don't let the title fool you. These are shifting and shifty fictions, artfully articulated cantilevers levered and buttresses flying. These are walls of sound in the wakes of spectacular wrecks! Here is the geological poetry of ice age glaciers gliding on their own tectonic melting."

—**MICHAEL MARTONE**, author of *The Complete Writing of Art Smith, The Bird Boy of Fort Wayne*, and *The Moon Over Wapakoneta*

"Jackson Bliss may have invented a new genre of fiction, call it hapa fiction. In this collection of genre-crossing stories, a Norwegian woman and Japanese man meet in a glass museum and give birth to a demigod glass blower. Gangs of tweens fight for racial justice on the streets of Grand Rapids. A lawyer vapes as she gazes longingly at the skyline of Tokyo while mixed-race kids left alone in Chicago compose songs from the notes blown by tugboats on the river. The realism in these stories is magical and Bliss makes the wonder that infuses them breezy as a jazz riff in a late-night Tokyo lounge. Or maybe it's Chicago."

—**STEVE TOMASULA**, author of *Once Human: Stories*

"A thrilling switchback roller coaster of a collection—by turns magical and absurd, nerdy and punk, soulful and furious. Read it/ride it—you'll have your hands in the air, your heart in your mouth, the wind in your hair!"

—**PETER HO DAVIES**, author of *The Fortunes* and
A Lie Someone Told You About Yourself

"This beautiful collection! Here are stories that challenge form, that attack the status quo, that ask urgent questions about love and identity and meaning and demand we sit up and pay attention to our answers. I left *Counterfactual Love Stories & Other Experiments* renewed and inspired. Jackson Bliss's boundary-pushing collection is an exquisite reminder that fiction, when written with this much heart and courage, can expand our understanding of what it means to be alive. You need to read this book."

—**JULIE BUNTIN**, author of *Marlena*

"There's an incredibly powerful attractive force waiting for you in every Jackson Bliss story, an irresistible magnetism powered by his energetic and welcoming voice, by his mathematical structural precision, by the wit and joy and justice that propel his fiction. This is one of the most inviting and innovative collections I've read, an endlessly compelling source of righteous adventure and wonder."

—**MATT BELL**, author of *Appleseed*

"Jackson Bliss sends the whole mixed-race, mixed-ability world spinning in these stories. Lucky for us, he has just the right besotted dream language to share his visions and just the right koans to satisfy our need for mystery. *Counterfactual Loves Stories & Other Experiments* is funny, provocative, and soulful—it's a wild ride and you should climb onboard."

—**VALERIE SAYERS**, author of *Brain Fever* and *The Powers*

"Energized and energizing, Jackson Bliss's *Counterfactual Love Stories* posits fusion and confusion as problem and possibility, from race, gender, and wealth inequality to genre, form, and perspective, all with an eye toward exploring how we might make meaning(s) out of our illegible, hyperbolic now. Every sentence is a surprising and sometimes vulnerable, sometimes satiric bite, data-dense as a shockwave ride through some video game committed to showing us what five minutes into our future will look like."

—**LANCE OLSEN**, author of *My Red Heaven* and *Skin Elegies*

COUNTER

LOV

E X

NOEMI PRESS

JACKSON BLISS

FACTUAL STORIES & OTHER RIMENTS

Cover and interior design by Alban Fischer

Published by Noemi Press, Inc.

A Nonprofit Literary Organization

www.noemipress.org.

この本をおばあさんに
捧げます。
真心こめて感謝します。

CONTENTS

CONSPIRACY OF LEMONS

Even before the first shot was fired, the security guard knew it was going to be a very long day. Before the insurrection on Halloween, he considered himself an atheist and a cynic, but there are some things too hard to understand, things without precedent, and one of them is a polished ten-inch Colt Python Revolver pointed directly up your nostrils. It wasn't every day that the Old Liberty Bank was heisted by a group of tweens in matching Catholic school uniforms and cowl, CEO, and Les Mis masks, appearing out of nowhere like a flash mob, their scrawny forearms barely strong enough to aim their weapons. Michigan wasn't Sierra Leone after all, but somehow the little bank robbers knew how to click the safety with their thumbs just like child soldiers.

Several hours later, a large clan of white kids in karate uniforms and red headbands raided the local Toys "R" Us, wielding Sai Swords in the air like religious fanatics. As the police report proved later on, the kids were professionals. They had magical powers that vaporized everything in their path like mushroom clouds, stuffing stolen SpongeBob backpacks with Nintendo Switches, Vita Games, fluorescent beach balls, Transformers, plastic chemistry beakers, Black Panther Lego sets, fruit-scented markers, and Michigan Monopoly boards. Even their getaway was impressive. It was a masterpiece of synchronicity with tiny battery-powered ATV's, Big Wheels, and those annoying electric scooters. By the time the police arrived, the toy store looked like something out of the hyper-real apocalypse. Aisles were covered in plastic snakes, white Barbie accessories and cat-eye marbles, bright whirling sound tubes and glittery hula-hoops. A sprained ankle at every turn. Eventually, the cops found the employees in the back, tied to a septic pipe with red karate belts and gagged by orange-striped tube socks. Next to seven empty cash registers, they discovered a pile of cell phones on the floor with the SIM cards removed and a heist note that no one noticed until later on in the investigation.

Sweet Dreams candy shop was the third place to get hit that night. There were rows and rows of emptied Mason jars normally filled with licorice wheels, taffy bow-ties, caramel dashes, sugar ellipses, spiraling lollipop drill bits, and glistening fruit-shaped marzipan. When the owner of Sweet Dreams arrived early the next morning, there was a supernova in his store window and a half-inflated basketball on the floor covered in fragments of glass and Wolverine-colored jelly beans. The till was missing, of course, and there was a pyramid of upside-down Mason jars on the floor. For some inexplicable reason, though, the marshmallow Peeps were still in the window. Their sugary beaks stared down the road like silent witnesses to a crime that hadn't been solved yet.

The fourth robbery wasn't discovered until the day after Sweet Dreams. When the manager of Wal-Mart unlocked the loading garage, he spilled his to-go cup in disbelief, which striped his khakis and burned his thighs with steamed milk. He couldn't believe his eyes. The entire electronics section—every plasma screen, Apple Watch, and laptop, every single iPhone 12 Pro, Bluetooth speaker, and Nintendo Switch—was gone. Not to mention all the hip-hop posters, tortilla chips, and Slim Jim canisters. Every pair of LeBron 18s. The whole shelf of Sunny D. And every *Euphoria* box set. Simply by making a tally of the merchandise, the manager knew what age the thieves were. He tried making a call to headquarters in Arkansas, his crotch smelling of sweet foam, when he noticed a note tacked to one of the HD television boxes. He tucked away his phone, removed his glasses, and pieced together the words. They were foreign-sounding, lacking verbs, and vaguely menacing. Then he called the police department. He had a thing or two to tell the sheriff about the Conspiracy of Lemons.

The part-time security guard forgot his gun again—it happens—so he stored his cell phone in the holster instead. You can't tell anyways from a distance. A bulge is a bulge. But when a phalanx of teenagers marched inside the lobby dressed like the Crazy 88 and heisted the bank like a conflation of two Quentin Tarantino movies, he was caught off guard. No pun intended. The security guard tried to lunge for one of their revolvers from behind a towering Ficus tree when a freckled Black girl dressed in a short jean skirt, "Ok Boomer" t-shirt, and Lehman Brothers CEO mask, blasted him in the foot. She shook her head in disapproval.

The guard howled in pain.

—Sir, please don't touch the gat, she hissed, pointing the gun at his nose.

—Little girl, he said, you don't wanna do this.

—Hell *yes* I do, she said, adjusting her mask.

—You can walk away from this right now if you want to.

· —Excuse me sir, shouted a Latino boy in a Countrywide CEO mask from an adjacent teller with a horrendous farmer's tan, —please stop talking or I'll have to shoot your other foot.

—Okay, okay, the guard reassured them. He put his hands up.

—Listen, buddy, a mixed-race girl said, turning her head around the perimeter and back to him, —this isn't the Iraq War or the George Floyd protests, so we don't run over innocent civilians.

—Huh?

As they spoke, the tellers moved back and forth between the vault and the getaway bags, feeding hundred-dollar bricks to gaping pillowcases until there was enough cold hard cash for the robbers to buy the Neverland Ranch from foreclosure or produce a Hollywood blockbuster with dazzling special effects. Meanwhile, the security guard applied pressure to his foot, the blood gurgling up like a stabbed juice box. When the bleeding stopped, he was going to press the emergency response button on his walkie-talkie. He had been waiting his whole life to press that thing.

The Grand Rapids police department had never seen so much crime before and what was worse, they had no leads either. The eyewitness testimony was flawed: not a single person—including the sheriff—had gotten a clean look at the bank robbers without their masks. Even worse, the Toys "R" Us employees didn't recognize the karate kids at all. It was as if they'd come from a secret village underground. And the security cameras at Wal-Mart, Old Liberty Bank, and Sweet Dreams, had all been spray-painted by a Native girl with pigtails and Gavroche mask. Another complication: the kids in this neighborhood were all multiracial. In smaller cities in Michigan, racial homogeneity had always been the easiest and most discriminatory technique to separate locals from non-locals. But when it came to making positive IDs for unsolved crime-sprees, the Grand Rapids police department had no forensics department. And Lansing wasn't sending in their strapped science geeks with the Q-Tips and DNA kits until dead bodies started popping up like spring dandelion clocks. Minh, the Kent County sheriff, had no alternative but to schedule a town hall meeting in November. And much to his surprise and annoyance, not a single person showed up, not even the old fogies, and they showed up for everything as long as there were snacks. Having no other choice, Sheriff Minh launched an ambitious door-to-door investigation that yielded troubling and contradictory evidence. A hint of conspiracy lingered in the air like stale lemons.

The manager from Wal-Mart took a cup of coffee from the receptionist at the police station—three cubes of sugar, three squirts of Half and Half—as he waited. Sheriff Minh entered the lobby. He was a chubby, balding, Asian American man with a permanent napkin tucked into his collar and a chuckle dabbed on his rosy cheeks.

—What can I do for you, Charlie? he asked, shaking his hand and waving him into his office.

—Minh, it's about the Conspiracy of Lemons.

—Oh, that, he said. He sat down and threw his napkin on the desk.

—Have you seen this? the manager asked, sliding the paper across the desk.

The sheriff scanned the note, a slow confusion accumulating on his face:

Brioche? Demands: Dads. Planet. Class. Bullshit Bomb.
Child. Yourselves. *fist drawing*

—Where'd you get this? he asked.

—In the loading annex.

—Brioche, huh?

—Is that a misspelling of brooch?

—Why brooch?

—I think it's a code.

—You think the word brooch is code?

—Terrorists speak in *code*. Everyone knows that.

—*I* didn't know that.

—Maybe it's time you called the feds. They know all about *terrorist* codes.

This comment stung the sheriff. He didn't like the idea of the FBI swooping down on his city and ripping the case out of his hands. It had to do with his pride, his staunch opposition to Islamophobia, and maybe a little with federalism. —All right, well, thanks for coming down, Charlie.

—They're trying to take over this country, he said, standing up.

—Who's they? Minh asked, trying his best not to sound accusatory over a xenophobic catchphrase he'd heard used against his family a million times after they'd arrived from Vietnam with the help of refugee resettlement services.

—The Islamofascists.

Minh sighed. —Give your wife my regards, he said, standing up and ushering him through the door with a shake of his head.

For the next week, the sheriff and a few of his deputies began a charm offensive. They chatted casually with the neighbors, trying to pry information one door at a time. Unfortunately, every household had a different theory as to what was causing the Conspiracy, expanding the number of explanations the department had been trying so hard to narrow down. The Menckens, for example, thought the Conspiracy of Lemons was a question of moral anarchy: how could parents spend time with their kids when they were pushing forty-hour weeks with no benefits, just to pay the bills? There wasn't enough light of day for family or moral instruction, so it wasn't a big surprise that kids were learning all the *wrong* values. They had no one guiding them, no one teaching them Leviticus. And, by the way, the Voses were a bunch of liberal traitors, Mr. Mencken warned, before slamming the door in his face. For the Díazes, both professors at Kalamazoo College, the problem was the sublimation of material identity, whatever that meant: advertising firms were spending millions of dollars trying to inject affluenza into our bloodstreams, deliberately targeting kids because they're *pervious* to masculinist hero culture, Mr. Díaz said, foaming at the mouth. Commercials are cultural propaganda anyway, the foxy Mrs. Díaz pointed out, a social mechanism to create consumers out of thin air by converting our own sense of inadequacy into an insatiable need for product consumption. And by the way, Mr. Díaz interjected, the Menckens are a bunch of cowfucking rednecks. The sheriff raised his eyebrows. The Andersons, on the other hand, said the Conspiracy was a product of atheism in America. People weren't afraid of God anymore and they *sure* weren't afraid of sin. Instead of going to church, kids were fiddling with fancy video game consoles and expensive cell phones while the rest of the rust belt was on its knees, praying for salvation before the apocalypse. Even worse, Mrs. Anderson confided, video games these days were so violent, sinful, and godless. Minh nodded politely, realizing he still needed to finish *Detroit: Become Human* before his son overrode his game (he was a dick when it came to video games). Just look at the Díazes, Mr. Anderson interjected, a bunch of shi shi liberals thumbing their noses at the world with their Ivy-League degrees, fake bilingualism, and highfalutin words. Finally, there were the outspoken Voses, who said the problem was the rich-poor gap. Rich kids were flaunting their SUVs, five-hundred-dollar purses, and iPhones to the world while down-and-out folks held up their pants with shoestrings.

—Of course, I'm all for integrated schools, he said, but they're *dripping* with class conflict.

—He's secretly a Commie, she said, laughing.

—Is that so? the sheriff sighed, trying to stifle his memories of the purges, disappearances, and assassinations that took place inside his village. —I didn't know that about you, Frank.

—No, Missy's full of shit, he said, I just want the world to be fair. And you know what? It's not. Rich people don't give a shit about poor people *or* their crappy schools, so poor people go and mug rich people so they don't feel powerless.

—Oh boy, here we go again, she said.

—Heard this before, have you? the sheriff asked.

Mrs. Vos raised her eyebrow and nodded.

—Look, Mr. Vos continued, I'm just saying: rich white people get scared, so they ask politicians to pass tougher laws for nonwhite people, which they do because they want campaign contributions. So, petty criminals stay in prison until they become professional criminals, rich white people build walls around their homes, install security cameras, and hire bodyguards.

Meanwhile, poor students of color in crappy school districts have no professional mobility because their broken-down, militarized schools don't prepare them for college so they work at gas stations or work across town in low-wage jobs that haven't been livable in sixty years or they deal drugs and end up as permanent members of the prison industrial complex. Then, rich white people get new laws passed to keep poor non-white people further away from their jewelry—all of this, just to make rich white people feel safe. And they *never* feel safe, that's the rub.

—That's quite a history lesson, the sheriff said.

—I'm just saying, Minh, a part of me, a *big* part of me, doesn't give a damn about our kids—

—Our kids, or your kids?

—I mean *all* of our kids.

—Just checking.

—I could give a damn if our kids are stealing shit right now when we're at the brink of a national catastrophe with this emotional, petty, vindictive, deeply narcissistic, intellectually deficient, sexual predator and pathological liar in chief.

—Okay, I think we get the point.

—I'm just saying, Mr. Vos continued, I don't blame kids for wanting justice in this fucked up world, I don't blame them for wanting more than we gave them, this system's made for us to spend money and die. That's it!

—Is that so? the sheriff asked.

—Of course. Kids are the victims in a dehumanizing economic system we stuffed down their throats. If you want to blame anyone, blame *us*. Don't blame the kids, Minh.

The sheriff nodded politely, shaking hands with the Voses before he handed them his card, just in case they saw anything suspicious in the future. Then he walked back to the police station, his mind now a thick muddle of words he vowed to Google back at home after he'd turned on his PS4.

The manager of the toy store didn't find the second note until the day after the bank robbery. It had been pinned on the floor underneath a magazine belt of Crayolas and naked Hollywood Kens, a hand-painted flag rubberbanded to their waists that read: *Whiteness = system of oppression.* The sheriff was drinking his second cup of coffee—oat milk, no sugar—when one of his deputies handed him the second note:

Mangent Are Back Killing Us Time A Is Get L

The sheriff shook his head and sipped his working-class café au lait. The second ransom note was gibberish. What in God's name was a mangent? Was this a misspelling of *magnet*? Or was it two words: *man* and *gent*? What the hell was a man gent anyway? And what if the real secret of the two notes was just bad orthography? What was he supposed to do then, put a grammarian on the payroll?

The sheriff decided to call Mr. Vos. He was a notorious blowhard and probably a secret elitist, but at least as a union man he spoke conspiracy theory fluently. The sheriff felt like he was running out of time and ideas whereas Mr. Vos seemed to be drunk on both. The sheriff drove his shiny new cruiser to their house, shook hands with Mr. Vos, and accepted ladyfingers and coffee from his wife. Once the two men were alone, the sheriff pulled out the second ransom note. Mr. Vos nodded his head like a Talmudic scholar as he scanned the words.

The sheriff bit one of ladyfingers, sugar crystals exploding on his lap, and then shifted positions. —Have any idea what that is?

—It's a manifesto.

—For what?

—For the abolishment of the 40-hour workweek. Or maybe a livable wage.

—Huh. That's what the Menckens said.

—The *Menckens?* Mr. Vos asked in horror. They're a bunch of Scripture nematodes.

The sheriff shrugged his shoulders.

At the front door, they shook hands quickly, but sadly, too.

The security guard was counting his bad luck. First, he forgot his gun, which was the biggest mistake of his damn life. His stepfather's voice echoed through his head, *from my cold dead hands*, which made him feel like a real dumbass. Then, the bank got heisted by kids in rented Catholic School uniforms and creepy masks of white guys, and they had *real* guns that could detonate his genitals or pin a piece of his lung to a bulletin board three hundred feet away. Kids weren't supposed to have that kind of power: they're too young to understand the value of life, the story behind every human subtraction. But even scarier, even if the security guard had brought his never-fired handgun, he still wouldn't have stood a fucking chance against the Flaming Red Hot posse. The emasculation of his authority as the only adult man in the lobby made him light-headed. At the twilight of his consciousness, he disconnected his walkie-talkie from his chest clip and slowly pulled it inside his pocket, stretching the coiled wire as far as it would go. He pretended to cough and pressed the red emergency button in a satisfying click that instigated his hope and salvation. Then, he passed out, the pain in his foot finally overwhelming him.

As the sheriff and his deputies made the rounds through Grand Rapids, they accumulated a formidable stack of theories about the Conspiracy of Lemons jotted down on crumpled notepads and recorded in twenty types of penmanship. It was impossible to know where to start, but also easy too because all their leads were anecdotal, flawed, and specious—an insatiable matrix of circumstantial evidence leading to nowhere.

As Minh reviewed his notes, his own theories about what happened seemed more unlikely but more realistic too. The Rodriguezes, for example, thought the problem was that American families didn't spend enough time together, just look at the Menckens. With the O'Connors, the problem was affirmative action, just look at the Rodriguezes, who spent too much time with their kids and not enough time at work. The Durants said the problem was American forces in the Middle East and unmitigated police brutality against Black men, which sent away perfectly good fathers to fight a bullshit 10-year war and left innocent Black kids to the mercy of racist cops with power trips, no offense, Minh, leaving their spouses to play the role of both parents. The Clovers said the problem was the lack of patriotism, just look at those slithering traitors, the Durants, eating truffle French fries, gruyere crêpes, and croque monsieurs as they watched NFL games. The Blackwells argued that the problem was America's rugged indi-vidualism: too many drivers, not enough passengers. Just look at the gas-slut Clovers and their seven cars, some of which had to be parked on their lawn. Who could live like that forever? The Finkelsteins said the root of the issue was multiculturalism, which was ripping a hole in America's soul: children didn't know who they were anymore because people like the Blackwells told them they could be *anyone* they wanted to be. The theories kept piling on until the sheriff was buried in an avalanche of suspicion, shtick, and prejudice. Slowly, he looked at the Conspiracy differently. Minh wasn't condoning the heist— it was grand larceny after all—but it was becoming clear what had happened, and as an elected public official and promoter of the peace, empathy always got in the way of criminal prosecutions.

A week later, an insurance agent from Bloomfield Hills stopped by to inspect the store window of Sweet Dreams and write out a check for the damage. The owner of Sweet Dreams was cleaning the countertop when he discovered the third ransom note hidden underneath pink fire hoses of bubblegum and a few crushed piano keys of milk chocolate. At first, he mistook the note for something his son—what was that expression his teacher had used, the *slam* poet—had written: all pruned and odd-sounding, the T's crossed in the same way like a loop slashed with a razorblade. The words meant absolutely nothing to him, as much as he tried. He was an honest Serbian immigrant, hardworking, but also completely immune to art and literature. He knew he was holding onto cold hard evidence though and that fact alone piqued his interest:

De La Our Our This Art Is Silent Someone's Over M

He didn't get it. Why was the word *our* repeated twice? And when *wasn't* art silent? He drove to the police station and dropped off the note, wiping his hands of another teenage enigma.

The sheriff felt like he was trying to solve a jigsaw puzzle with literary analysis and he wasn't even sure the puzzle formed a coherent picture. Maybe the ransom notes were just a way of messing with adults who had rules, principles, and protocol. Kids were mischievous like that. Not to mention hyperactive, impulsive, and cruel as hell.

As a last resort, Minh called Mrs. Díaz and asked her to stop by after she returned from Kalamazoo. *Don't worry,* he said, *you're not in any trouble.* At quarter to five, she was sitting in his office with a cup of Chinese green tea on her lap that only Asians, liberals, and health fanatics asked for when they stopped by.

—Thanks for coming down, he said.

—No problem, she said with a nervous hint in her voice.

—I wanted to ask you something.

—Minh, it's just an occasional thing, I promise. One or two puffs at the most.

—What?

—Oh.

—What are you talking about?

—Isn't that why I'm here?

—No, it's not, so don't say another word. I *don't* want to know.

—Okay.

He shook his head. —Besides, it's been legal here forever. Where have you been?

—True, she said, exhaling, I guess it's just a habit. So, what can I do for you?

—Do you understand any of this? he asked, sliding the wrinkled ransom notes across the birch desk like a casino dealer.

Mrs. Díaz slipped on her glasses, the pink metal frames looking smart and vaguely European. She hunched over the desk to scrutinize the penmanship, tiny strands of blond hair falling down her profile, removing ten years in a flash of adolescence. Through the dusty blinds, her face looked radiant and soft. The sheriff thought about junior high, back when he'd had a secret crush on her, even though she was the class nerd and he was just a third-string defensive end trying to prove his patriotism through the sacrifice of his own Asian body. He looked at her with desperation, resurgent longing, and irrational hope, which made him feel ashamed.

She took a sip of tea. —It's poetry.

—Poetry?

—Yeah, probably Dadaist.

—How do you know that?

—The French is the giveaway. My French isn't what it used to be, but this line is easy to translate. It says: *They eat brioche*.

—When you say *brioche*, you mean—

—That eggy French bread that feels like you're nibbling on a delicious cloud?

—But what does bread have to do with the Conspiracy?

—That's just it. It's not supposed to mean anything. That's the whole point of Dada.

—Sounds like a crock of shit to me.

—A crock of shit is a *perfect* metaphor of Dada, actually.

—So, what you're trying to tell me is that all of this is supposed to be a work of art?

—Possibly. Or it could be a live semiotic text. Even performance art. Who knows? But those are just theories.

—Theories are all I've got right now.

—Well, theories are all you need in my field.

—Unfortunately, he said, sighing,—they don't satisfy grand juries like they used to.

———

Three days later, the sheriff called a professor of French lit at U of M to decode the first line, which, evidently, was a Marie Antoinette quote. Who knew? Once Minh understood the syntax of the French, he was able to work out the correct order of the ransom notes. The sheriff arranged the four notes into a coherent message and laughed. Even when kids were robbing banks, filling their pockets full of candy, and ripping off high-tech electronics, they were earnest little bastards. Too young to be indoctrinated by sarcasm or irony. Their sincerity, while misguided, was refreshing:

Qu'ils	Mangent	de la	Brioche?
These	Are	Our	Demands:
Bring	Back	Our	Dads.
Stop	Killing	This	Planet.
Give	Us	Art	Class.
Quality	Time	Is	Bullshit.
Poverty's	A	Silent	Bomb.
Everyone	Is	Someone's	Child.
Please,	Get	Over	Yourselves.
B	L	M	*fist drawing*

The first place to get robbed was the Old Liberty Bank, but it was also the sheriff's last piece of evidence, helping him "solve" the mystery of Grand Rapids' one and only documented child insurrection. By comparing alibis, video camera footage, and attendance logs at the public junior highs, he eventually concluded that every kid in the neighborhood had participated in at least one heist. Some, all four. Even worse, the kids' parents were all hiding something too. That's when Minh dropped the investigation. There was nothing he could do with two hundred defendants that wouldn't destroy his career and disparage the entire city. He refused to take down the only home he'd ever known.

In time, he learned to ignore the futuristic glow of sparkling smart TVs flashing through his neighbors' windows. He stopped asking them where they got the money to buy brand new iPhones and state-of-the-art desktop computers, family vacation packages to Cedar Point, and new dental implants for grandparents used to gumming their syllables for years. The people of Grand Rapids had never wanted him to ask too many questions, especially about their mysterious abundance of Christmas gifts that winter, and he really hated being lied to, so he stopped sticking his nose in people's inexplicable cash flow. Besides, he had a video game with forty-five endings to finish before his son erased everything.

After the security guard pressed the mythical red button and passed out, "The Star-Spangled Banner" blared over the bank's PA system in a monophonic clamor. The customers lying on the ground covered their ears, wincing. Thirty minutes later, the Fire Department showed up after a tween called 911 using a stolen SIM card. Ten blocks from the bank, the sheriff saw a multiracial group of kids in Catholic School uniforms and cowl, Les Mis, and CEO masks trick-or-treating (their guns tucked inside bulging pillowcases filled with Halloween candy and Dead Presidents).

Minh stopped his car and rolled down the window. —Who are *you* guys supposed to be?

—The Crazy 88, they all shouted, like duh!

The sheriff smiled and told them to be good. He hated Quentin Tarantino movies. Well, everything except *Pulp Fiction.* But there were worse directors to imitate. Right as Minh shooed them away, an armored SWAT van zipped by, fishing between cars stuck at the intersection. Minh looked at the tweens through his rearview mirror and chuckled. They were just kids after all and kids were always the victims, even when they were the ones pulling the trigger.

HEAVEN ABOVE

I. 六本木午前 3 時 (Roppongi at 3 am)

1. To read flash fiction about a man who does nothing but take showers all night inside love hotels and eat other people's leftovers in the fridge, go to page 169.

2. 時間があったら、327 ページをご覧ください。

II. Dying in the Past

3. To read flash fiction about two creepy hapa girls named Ko and Wai who do nothing but dress up in their mom's old '80s goth dresses and make music videos of themselves dancing to The Smiths, go to page 172.

4. To sit down on a bench in the Art Institute and quickly see your life in microcosm in Kandinsky's "Painting with a Green Center," a coincidence that probably feels too easy to be true, consider "Green is the Most Popular Letter" on page 65.

KOTHAR SHINKA

I. Divine Lineage

The first thing Kothar told me at his glassworks studio in Traverse City was that he came from a family of half-goddesses. His birth was a panegyric, he said: his Japanese dad and Norwegian mom met at a museum of glass in Oslo as they'd waited for a winter storm to pass. Eventually, they fell in love, moved to the mitten, and started a small nuclear family during the Cold War. Kothar said he had the seeds of illusion in him. He was—not to brag—an apotheosis, a conjurer of worlds. His birth name was Kothar-wa-Khasis Shinka, the god of Canaan, but his name could also be translated as *sagacious and adroit*, he pointed out. I almost walked away right then and there, but for some reason, I was captivated by his transparency and false grandeur.

II. Prophecy

Someday he would shatter my heart, Kothar told me. I said I would never let him get close enough to break anything. He smiled, shaking his head. He told me I would get my revenge. Someday, I would take away his art. Impossible, I thought. He's not an artist and I'm not a thief.

III. The Age of Magic

After I watched him blow glass that first time, I realized he was half-divine after all. With his lips, Kothar created an entire genesis out of thin air like a creator breathing life into empty vessels of flesh and shell. In a single night I watched him produce:

1. A cobalt blue glass merry-go-round that changed songs depending on the lighting

2. Children dressed in cowl masks, pointing their guns at a security guard

3. A glass replica of the Akershus Fortress that turned to jelly when touched

4. A crossword puzzle made with puffy, frosted Hiragana

5. A motel sign on US-31 that read *sleep here tonight, we beg you*

6. A replica of the ring monument at Vigeland Park that snowed whenever the room temperature fell below 59 degrees

7. A group of Geisha dolls, their bodies forming the kanji for *car accident*

8. A replica of the Oslo School of Architecture and Design intersecting with a snapshot of the Shinjuku skyline etched in a thin sheet of iridescent glass

9. An omega-shaped fishbowl, the lips of the goldfish open like pouty French teenagers confessing their love

10. A mirror that reflected your real, imagined, distorted, and ideal selves

11. A Mason jar filled with crystalized "miso"

12. A perfect replica of Chagal's *America Windows*

13. A collapsible Hanksen Museum of Sculpture that folded into a tiny square

14. A pair of golden Guccis missing their lenses

15. A juvie detention facility made in the shape of a glass knife, the prisoner, staring at you through the windows

16. A tiny miniature of me holding a brick in my hand

17. A mixed-race art student carrying a canvas tote of overdue library books

18. A replica of my heart, excessively detailed, the arteries swollen like bruised lips

IV. Call Me Wise-and-Perceptive

Kothar also means *wise and perceptive*, he explained.

Sure it does, I thought. If you're so wise and perceptive, what am I thinking? I asked him.

You're thinking, sure it does.

Wrong, I retorted, my face smeared in the clumsy stage make-up of pathological liars. Because he loved me and saw through my denial, he simply kissed my temples with lips that burned in silent aplomb and sloppy lust.

V. Architecture & Interior Design

The first time Kothar took me to his apartment on Front Street, I walked through the front door and laughed. There was no furniture except a queen-sized bed, a carpenter's table, three different sized furnaces, a cardboard box of tools—pliers, tongs, stuff for torturing his girlfriends I guess—and a yellow tapestry covered with a few musty dishes, wine glasses stained with purple lip marks, and a burnt pipe half-filled with bright red hash. I noticed a self-portrait mosaic of Kothar as a half-divine hapa boy staring out the window. I told him his studio was barren, inappropriate for a man of his skill and mismatched for a woman of my convictions. Three days later, when we returned from shopping for curtains from the Village, I walked inside and fell through the floor. Kothar's studio had been completely transformed into Kublai Khan's Palace. There was a glass fountain where the kitchen sink used to be, a bathtub carved of transparent minerals, a golden dining room table and glass chairs that looked embroidered in the rarest and softest fabric in all of the Silk Road. There were diaphanous bookcases filled with transparent books, each word chiseled into thin sheets of sparkling white glass paper. There were a series of glossy mirrors at the far end of the apartment that reflected the windows, expanding the bedroom, expanding the stars at night, multiplying space and time like a voracious multiverse. I gazed at the steel-reinforced glass canopy bed, blown in the shape of a giant wave, covered in Roma strands of bright and luxurious linen, protected by light green crystal statues of slender Odalisques, their legs frozen in the air. When Kothar turned the light switch on and off, the shadows of the Odalisques danced on the ceiling like shadow play.

VI. History

Kothar told me his views about history. He said that history was a circle of friable glass: it could be broken but not destroyed. It was fragile but predictable. It was protean but inert, relying on glassblowers to extract art from abstraction. History had no mind of its own but went on forever in a circle of flowing words and permutating numbers, he said. History was the very definition of metastability.

VII. Spells

Kothar said he knew how to cast spells.

Then cast one on me, I said.

I already have.

Well, it's not working. I dislike you more each day.

That's what I'd hoped for.

God, you piss me off.

Maybe it's working too well.

VIII. Hanging Gardens

I told him I was sick of living in a Harem and wanted an opulent garden instead. The next morning, I woke up shivering. As I rubbed my eyes, I thought I was lying on top of a mirage. Kothar had been busy the night before creating the Hanging Gardens of Babylon in his artisan guild. A thousand trees full of ripe, dripping, luscious glass fruit grew from tiny glass pots along the wall. But what I missed was Georgia Savannah and fermented marsh. I learned that day that I had to be precise with my words.

IX. Opener of Windows

At first, I thought Kothar was some rich miser who had simply bought all his glass furniture impulsively to impress me. I'm used to men going to great lengths to touch the covenant of my legs, trying to open them up like a mysterious ark. I assumed he hid bulbous stacks of cash underneath his mattress, waiting for war and hunger to strike. But every morning when it rained, he propped open the windows. He said he was helping Ba'al fertilize the earth. How seminal, I thought. How phallocentric, he said.

X. Translation

Once, at a Thai restaurant in Suttons Bay, I watched in jealous awe as Kothar told jokes in Thai to the waitresses. They began multiplying like faces in a department store mirror, forming a small circle around our table, their entranced eyes filled with frozen tears of entangled jubilation. They loved and adored him, melting into small droplets of laughter, evaporating onto the threadbare carpet like a small choir of deliquescent faces. In time, the small waitresses replaced each other and multiplied like new answers for the Hodge Conjecture, numbers permutated, bodies disappeared into the kitchen, returning with exquisite plates that were far too rich and complex for our vulgar appetites: Venezuelan dark chocolate, green Indian mangos and Bangkok red chili, blood limes, saffron threads, coconut rice, and white truffles, young coconut water served with spun sugar straws, portobello skewers drenched in peanut sauce, Royal Cardamon, and lemongrass oil. After he paid the bill, I asked him where he learned to speak Thai. He said that there was no such thing as primary language. Everything was a translation of something. I told him he meant corruption, though I knew they weren't the same thing. He said the name Kothar-wa-Khasis, the god of Canaan, could also be translated as *alternate translations*. I thought about grabbing his water glass and breaking it over his head, but I stopped myself when I thought of Kothar's first glass figurine of me, holding a brick in my hands. I'd never felt so manipulated by an artist before. Obviously, I didn't know enough artists.

XI. Music

In an attempt to bend his will, I gave Kothar orders all day long, just because: *Kothar, open the door for me and hold my dress. Kothar, make me oatmeal and make it sweet. Kothar, set my bath and make the top layer of water tepid. Kothar, go out and buy more Japanese chocolate sticks. Kothar, go down on me and stay there until I come.* I expected him to defy me, which would be a pretext for a drawn-out fight. I thought he would stand his ground like a giant admiring the acceleration curve of stones launched from a teenager's slingshot, but he followed my every whim, smiling only for himself. The more he obeyed me, the more I wanted to bite his face off. I wanted him to resist and he wasn't playing along, so I lied on my hardwood floor and started grinding my teeth. I would not open up to him. My shoulders ached from tension, my teeth became a sparkling white powder, and I could feel him laughing behind my back. I hated him with my nails and my elbows and my lungs and my thighs. I vowed to hate-fuck him the first chance I got. I would break his heart someday, smashing his Sultan's Chamber with a croquet hammer. The glass would be a rare melody of violence.

XII. Magic Words

The problem with Kothar was that he always drugged me with his art, his eyes, and his language. Each euphonious sentence was a tiny particle of mescaline, building up in my brain until I was living in his psychedelic dream world. When, out of the blue, I accused him of using me, he dropped the dishes he was hand-drying on the glass floor and sprinted to the bed, suffocating me with his warm sweet skin and dense bone mass. Those splintered plates were the sweetest stanzas he'd ever recited to me.

XIII. Lost City

Kothar told me that his favorite city was called Kaphtor.

Where is that?

It doesn't exist anymore. It was erased by war and cartography.

So, it's an illusion?

Kaphtor is an idea, like all ancient cities.

Are we a city?

We're an idea, if that's what you mean.

It's not.

XIV. The Masseur

Before I could ask him for a massage, Kothar undressed me on his new glass bed (the Wave of Kanagawa) that he'd blown last week during his Hokusai phase. He unzipped my defiance and defensiveness, plying my entangled wires with skilled and precise fingers, pulverizing my knots into small diamond fragments until he'd bruised my shoulder blades and ripped the tension out of my stiff muscles like an anchor windlass. I told him his fingers were the sexiest part of his body. He laughed, bending over and whispering into my ear his secret: Kothar can also be translated as *skilled hands or self-multiplying fingers*. I shook my head until it jingled.

———

XV. Egyptian Memphis

Once, as we drank lattes on a plaid picnic blanket in the Commons, Kothar told me his second favorite city after Traverse City was Memphis.

Memphis? How in the world have you visited Tennessee?

I mean the Memphis of ancient Egypt. The first one.

I didn't know there was a precursor.

Cities are just a space of interconnected ideas. Cities are just slow translations of history. Cities are just monuments of protest against the Angel of Death.

You've already told me your theory. More than once, actually.

Then you understand why I love a city that doesn't exist.

Actually, I still don't.

You love me and yet we're just an idea.

I hate you.

Hatred is a metropolis. A grid with a million streets of pain.

I slapped him and then apologized in a text.

XVI. Second Translation

One night, as we were falling asleep on his giant wave bed, I asked Kothar why he became an artist. He explained that glass-blowing allowed him to translate his inner world into materiality and materiality into art. That was the only way he knew how to love me, he explained, by translating me into fragments of frozen light, which he said he could never capture. His admissions of failure were always the pathway of flattery for me.

XVII. Fraud

There is a special rage that white women have towards talented men who make them feel bad about themselves, even when that rage is the bloom of their own insecurity, resentment, malice, privilege, and jealousy. Kothar was one of those men and I was one of those women. In fact, the more attractive, generous, and kind he became, the more I detested him, ranting about him to anyone who would listen. A big part of me wanted to open him up and show the world what a giant egomaniacal fraud he was. When I told him I would one day expose him to the world, he said his only job was to make art out of broken people and love them, even during their collapse. I tried to slap him as hard as I could, just to see him break. He caught me by the wrist and kissed my palm until I cried angry tears.

XVIII. Age

One day at a Karaoke bar in Novi, I'd asked Kothar how old he was. He said he was old enough to watch glass slowly flowing through the fingers of eternity. I said yeah right and slammed my shot glass on the counter. Kothar stroked my hand, making tiny swirls with his fingertips on the tense archway of my veins, and then the shot glass turned to liquid before my eyes. I shook my head and slapped the magic trick out of his hand. The shot glass became solid again and split into a million pieces. Kothar smiled and said, *If this isn't art, then tell me what is.* Then he got up on stage and sang "Living on a Prayer" to an enraptured audience of Japanese housewives who threw twenty-dollar bills at his feet, which I collected to buy cab fare home.

IX. Myth

Last night Kothar cheated on me. It was subtle, but it sliced me into islands. We were making love, his body infecting mine, when I saw him looking through the window. Instead of looking at me, instead of adoring me, he was looking away, looking at himself in the window, looking at the infinity of his own bedroom, multiplied by glass and mirror. He was looking at everything, his own face, my unwrapped body, the apartment buildings across the street, their ocean blue interior, exposed heating ducts, and loft ceilings. He was looking at everything at once, in love with his neighborhood and with the refraction of halogen lamps from apartment windows. He was in love with liquid glass and frozen light, Pi and Fibonacci, color theory, additive, and reflection.

XX. Theft

I know what I did was wrong, but once I get revenge in my bloodstream, I just need to release it before it consumes me. I recognize my prophetic vengeance for what it is and I take responsibility for my violence. Throwing a brick through a studio window is never a smart idea, even if it belongs to your cheating ex-boyfriend who seduced you with his stories of metamorphosis, divine lineage, and artistic creation. But after I hurled that brick at shelves and shelves of glass figurines crammed from wall to wall and floor to ceiling inside his studio, after I shattered his stories of glass, his winters of color, all waiting inside their trenches of darkness and neon, I wanted to destroy Kothar's mythology and transform his inert ideas into useless desires again. My violence, just as he'd predicted, was simply my declaration of love, written to him in terms only he could identify, a translation of rage only he would understand the next day when he returned from his obāchan's funeral like a prince reeking of tragedy.

UNRELIABLE DESTINIES TO NOWHERE

1. To watch a divine glassblower stop time, go to KOTHAR'S AFTER HOURS (p. 306).

2. To read a story without a story, a text without a text, go to 10 MORE KOANS (p. 200).

3. To witness a narrator floating through the walls, go to THE PERMEABLE MEMBRANES OF OUR LIVES (p. xvi).

4. To listen to an audio version of this conceptual short story collection, go to READING IS A FORM OF DREAMING (p. 600,000,000,000, 000,000,000,000,000,000,000,000).

SECRET CODES &
OPPRESSIVE HISTORIES

1.

From the train windows, Ann Arbor looks airbrushed by a lush and bountiful acrylic mist, at least until the train passes the outskirts and the sun slowly eats away at the lingering murk. **He** doesn't miss A2 yet because he can't imagine being anyplace else. He looks through the window at wobbly houses near the tracks where rusty pickup trucks, overturned recycling bins, and hand-me-down bikes have sunk into soggy grass lawns. He **loves** the lullaby of the quiet train, the way the sun drills large holes through a pageant of clouds. He loves the endless parishes of trees, which remind him of the outskirts of Tokyo, the idea of Tokyo always larger than the city itself (just like Ann Arbor). He loves **the** basic **idea of** nature, the open space, the clean lyricism of the sky. It's easy to **love** something you don't have to commit to. Besides, three days is hardly a vacation. Barely enough time to exhale, really. **But** his daughter asked him to visit her in Chicago for the first time in fifteen years and he jumped on the first available Amtrak with a reserved coach ticket in his yellow hands that were wrinkled by four divorces and discolored by thirty years of smoking. He'd been waiting for the slightest peep, the slightest spark of communication from her since the day Shizuko changed her address and phone number without warning. She didn't even give him the simplest sentence conjunction. It was **only** after his fourth wife passed away from breast cancer and a gingered liver that Shizuko invited him to her survivalist cottage. And really, that was the first time he wanted to go see her again.

2.

When you were a little girl riding with your otōsan, you always preferred the backseat. Up front, you were a forced guide: you helped with directions, unfolding each layer and imaginary story from the state map, you reconnoitered crucial information and counted exits, you negotiated radio stations and numbers for the heating fan, **when** you were cold you lobbied for 4, but 4 was wasteful, Dad said, sliding the heat to 3. His fists were always smoking, clenching the steering wheel as a cigarette burned between his knuckles. The front seat was mythological, like a Genji tale, the place where his fists blanched and smoked like brimstone, always merciless, pruned of shadow and devoid of vertigo. **He** had always been that way. Sitting shotgun was a lot of work without any power, especially for a young girl obsessed with romance manga, Atom bomb survivors, and number theory.

3.

Fifteen years **is** a long time, long enough to reinvent your hapa daughter or pretend she died in the Sunni Triangle fighting in an illegal war she knew you hated after she'd enlisted. Long enough to bury the old photo albums in the attic and drag them back out again when he was between wives and hardpacks. Now, he's **afraid** she will look older than he does. Gin, children, PTSD, and canned food will do that to you. The truth is, he couldn't stand Shizuko's militia husband, his penchant for conspiracy theories, and his weird anti-vaxxing opinions: teaching their kids to hunt, fish, and fire rifles before they knew how to spell their own names, forcing them to use candles instead of electricity, the radio instead of the TV, dressings the boys in camouflage and combat boots, homeschooling them in bear traps, wilderness survival, field leadership, Christianity, shoe polish, and trench warfare. What the hell kind of *education* was that? He felt personally responsible for every mistake Shizuko made in her life, but he still wanted her in his life, at least tangentially. Her dreary husband, however, didn't approve **of** her blunt father, the Karate Sensei and the Iraq War critic. She made a choice and goddammit, it was the wrong one.

4.

In the backseat, you had no rights, no responsibilities, no pathologies as a mixed-race Japanese girl. You didn't even exist, except as a voice **disjointed** from your body, your words floating abstractly towards the dashboard like little balloons, popping above the gas gauge. This is the time you loved the most: in motion, between exits and **state** lines, between black dots on fold-up **maps**. You were normally calm and unaffected, the way all ignored passengers were. You didn't mind this at all. The car window was a television set, a portal to the transient and fleeting world like riding in a Humvee through Baghdad. You liked reading highway signs, you liked the way they advertised other people's stories and created an alternative life for you inside your head. You admired the blur of farmland **and** sunset, sticky traffic lights and cut-and-dry coastlines, **swollen** hills and battered tarmac sky during the solemn drizzle of cold rainy mornings.

5.

He doesn't know what the hell he's gonna see in Chicago. A stretched-out, burned-up, conspiracy-whispering Shizuko? A beer-bellied Rambo wannabe, dressed in camouflage shorts and a "Lock Her Up" t-shirt, dragging who-knows-how-many slave kids to the front door? Will her family look like a group of lost mixed-race angels? A rabid militia? Will they look like a Gorian cult? An upstart Waco? Nothing would surprise him at this point. Shizuko had always been a sensitive, forgiving, and observant girl, and maybe that was his fault. Maybe, he pressed his hard-nosed cultural politics down her throat one too many times at the dinner table. Maybe, he should have listened more or encouraged her to think for herself. Maybe, instead of making her read Mishima, *The **Tales** of Genji,* and Kenzaburo Oe as a teenager, he should have gone to her high school softball games and hugged her when she misspelled "psoriatic" in the regional Spelling Bee, bursting into tears on local TV. But no, he'd been consumed by his failing relationships, his silent hierarchies of value, and his karate tournaments. He offered her no opportunities in which she could assert her own genius or discover her own pride or pry open her **grief**. He thought that was her responsibility. Still does, in fact. He's always had a hard time not justifying his own shitty behavior.

6.

Somewhere along the way to adulthood, you made a promise to yourself never to drive as long as you lived, which included the back roads of Iraq. There were already too many drivers in America and not enough passengers. Besides, you were a miserable copilot: you preferred radio plays and AM talk shows (the crazier the better), you gazed at nature **between** your otōsan's sentences, you'd always been a silent kid, always drunk on shots of sugar and sunset. But in the backseat, you understood the difference between an early morning and a late night. You knew how to count overpasses, bird migrations, bike gangs, and **hazmat** trucks on I-475. You loved the **rain** when the heat was cranked up to 3, though 4 always felt like Mom's home before she cheated on Dad **and** moved to Peoria to live with a casino dealer who called himself El Silver Fox on social media, a man who was neither geriatric nor Spanish speaking. You knew the difference between a rest stop, a flat tire, and a sleazy budget motel that practically made you Shinto. There was something about the energy of highways, headlights streaking your face, the powder **blue** moon peeking through your window, something about eating farmer omelets and sausage patties at a musty **diner** on the side of the road, something about listening to Otis Redding in the late afternoon when the **tequila** sunlight melted your insides as you looked through **the** rear windshield, hugging yourself in the fading light, that felt almost divine in retrospect.

7.

As the sun bows it head, prostrating golden arms on the altars of ancient forests and blighted industrial zones, sunlight pours into the train like a divine overflow, bouncing off the blue leather interior, **blinding** passengers in the spaces between towns, the thin sharp flickers of light becoming an aggravated assault of **splendor.** On the wrong side **of paradise** and struck by the sun's spotlight, he **feels** old and exposed, **divorced from** nature, divorced from his childhood in Chiba and his senior years in Novi, divorced from a world he doesn't even understand.

Fifty miles from Chicago, he has to admit that he would take a three-month girlfriend any day of the week over his long-lost daughter, meeting **the** minutemen, or learning to set goddamn bear traps in the **prairie**. He loves his daughter just fine from a critical distance because he doesn't have to commit to fatherhood and its oppressive historiographies. But in a run-down motel on US-31, in a strange apartment building, **and** in a rusty, fogged-up mustang, the cheap drink rising from their middle-aged skin like engine fumes, he knows how to survive just fine inside a woman's arms. He's a survivor of history, just like Shizuko. If nothing else, he taught her that. **The** problem has always been that they've never fought the same **war**.

ASTRAL PROJECTION SEQUENCE

After binging on *A Silent Voice, Euphoria, Fleabag, Choose-Your-Own-Adventure Novels, RTJ4,* and *Borderlands 3* for hours and hours, you become trapped inside your own mind. Eventually, your spirit disconnects from your body and travels via astral projection to:

1. A sunglass store in Lakeview: HOW TO NOT FIND LOVE WITH YOUR FAKEASS GUCCIS (p. 93).

2. A boutique in the Gold Coast that sells overpriced organic hoodies: SOLA'S ASTERISK (p. 113).

3. A sports bar in Detroit filled with drunk bros arguing about NFL teams and other topics saturated in Social Darwinism: ENTRANCE EXAM TO MY HEART (p.149).

4. A shopping mall in Montréal, where two beautiful men dressed in giant GOLDFISH COSTUMES, become obsessed with la viande fumée (p. 337).

FOURTEEN SONGS
FOR THE STEERING WHEEL

1. "Ricochet"

Ali Suzuki had legs made of copper that ricocheted sunlight and shimmied from woodblock waves to pastel beach towels in quiet fluidity. After her boyfriend's Neon, the one with the hand-installed spoiler, collided into a minivan of kids in basketball jerseys, her yoga instructor legs dangled out the passenger window like a beautiful disaster. They were the only thing you could bear to look at, if you had the nerve, I mean, to keep on looking at another hit and run on I-94.

2. "Diction of Stars"

I said I wouldn't touch him down there, but he pleaded like a fuckboy, even tried to plop my hand on his hard-on like I was a human blanket he could just throw over his lap to cover up his embarrassment and protect him from the wind that smacked the windows in disapproval. We were parked on a cliff in South Haven. I was watching furious waves engulf a tiny red lighthouse and Marty O'Brian was all over me like a marine layer. When I realized he wouldn't stop and I wouldn't get away, I pulled up my shirt and let him touch my breasts. He rubbed and fondled them like they were pieces of dough, kneading them into random shapes: a question mark, a coconut, a popsicle. When he was done, I handed him a Kleenex like he asked and went outside on the bluffs to watch the stars blinking like idea clusters. They were a series of dots and dashes in the horizon, as if intergalactic operators on the other side of the universe were sending us desperate telegraphs from the void. When Marty drove away, I didn't cry. I was finally alone. The breeze rushed at my face and the smell of the air was a pungent trance of summer. I spent a good hour looking up at the sky before I realized that dying stars (like human beings) have their own swan song. They make their last declarations in code using the slow violence of the sky as a switchboard. I started to wonder, as the wind punched me between the eyes: how many times do these sidereal messages go unread and did anyone ever read them before they were gone?

3. "Break the Fast"

There she is in the back seat, burning like a paper cut. Each day, Savarna stands at the corner of Addison and inner Lake Shore Drive. As if guided by instinct, I would discover her there, her arm dangling above her head like a dejected sunflower. What seemed first like cosmic coincidence was quickly demystified: we were creatures of habit and our bodies responded to tragedy with consistency. For months, I picked her up each morning at 7:48 a.m. and all my attempts at small talk failed miserably. While her saris and kurtas changed pattern and luminosity, her face remained unaffected by our awkwardness. In the rearview mirror, I saw my own daughter rising up from the ashes like a splintered avatar. Now, the tightness in her lips betrays the contained radiance of her cheekbones, her sadness weaponizing the air like fried pepper. The worst part is I have to pretend I don't understand her pain. Last week, after getting ripped off and threatened by a white man in a black suit who told me to go back from where I came from, I parked at Paresh's 7-Eleven on Waveland and discovered Savarna curled up in the alley like a question mark. Her hands clung to her knock-off purse, the blood on her lips had coagulated into smashed mulberries, one of her eyes was swollen like a new moon, a long, trailing river of pink snot dribbled onto her face, and her royal sari had shoe prints on it, the sleeves demoted to crude swatches. I picked her up in my arms and laid her down in the backseat of my taxi as gently as I could before looking for her wallet. I drove her home, even though she lived two blocks away. As I unlocked the front door of the building, one of her neighbors passed me in the hallway, her eyes scanning me in binary. She tried to figure out if I was the kind of Indian who helped women or the kind who silenced them. Inside her apartment, she spoke to the police in a frantic whisper. I kicked the front door of Savarna's apartment open with my sandals, walked down the hallway, unlocked her apartment, and carried her to her sofa upholstered with embroidered cedars. She snored in my arms like a precocious niece, the story of her life wheezing out of her. She was a world I had no business knowing. After I laid her down and covered her with a throw whose color eluded me, I closed the door behind me. I wished I could have kept her keys and locked her door from the outside to protect her from the creeping injustice of this world, but she needed a way out. We all did.

Now, I look at Savarna in my taxi, wearing her Jackie O Gucci sunglasses that swallow her face like a spell. I guard my silence, never saying her name out loud. Like her sofa that matched her pillows, like the black and white photo of her family in London that hung in her hallway like a coat of arms, like her chipped vase decorated with elephants (their trunks curled into tiny commas just like Savarna's body the night she slept on wet cement like human punctuation), her name is forbidden knowledge. I cannot speak what I know. When I arrive at her office on Lakeshore Drive, I wait until she's paid and is almost to the revolving door of her building, her feet planted firmly on the sidewalk, and then, just before her hands touch glass, I thank her. And because the sky is dark and swollen like her left eye and because I have to blow her ashes away after holding on to them for days now, I say at last: —Have a nice day, Ms. Savarna. She stops in her tracks and turns around as if she heard me. All this time and I still don't know what her voice sounds like. At this point, any sound will do.

4. "Requiem"

Sometimes, when I'm in the passenger's seat and my boyfriend is driving to Dearborn, I'm tempted to grab the steering wheel and swerve into oncoming traffic on I-94. Just four inches, a hard left on the steering wheel separating life from death, restraint from release, decay from rebirth. In every daydream of mine, one perfect accident would void the authority of his biceps and cancel the violence of their curvature. I can see my limp body hanging out of the windshield, my tan arms dangling over the hood of my boyfriend's Neon like a heroin junkie showing off her drug stigmata. I can see his body as a hemorrhage of color, covered in a veil of splintered glass. I can see his fists melting in the burning sun like abandoned wax figurines. I want them reshaped into objects that can't break my skin or dislocate my shoulders or rip my bathing suit at a Vegas hotel swimming pool when I smile at a waiter out of loneliness when he asks me if I'm okay. I fantasize about car accidents because they can take the roar out of engines and the whiteness out of knuckles. They are requiems for all of us who keep on living in this dead life.

5. "Your Life Will Never Be the Same"

My okāsan told me being a limo driver was bad news: —If you wanna see how ugly white people can really be, then go ahead. If you wanna deal with drug-addicted movie stars and frowning men in fancy suits, divas and teenagers trying to pretend they're in a Gatsby narrative, then go ahead. I won't stop you, Kuma, but they will, and when they do, your life will change forever. I crossed the Michigan state line and started thinking as I drove through that blighted city of forgotten warehouses, why Mr. Cannello made me promise to lock the doors and not look in the trunk unless I wanted to lose my job and four fingers. He promised to break my manicured fingernails and I looked anyways. I took a peek. I'm only human, goddammit. I know what my okāsan would say if she saw this, she'd smack me across the head and drag me to the 75th Street Shinto Temple and force me to sing "The Song of Light," even though the light was always skipping over Asians. Still, how could I explain to the kami why there were thirty-five blue Bengali cubs, *endangered cubs,* as the papers pointed out later that summer, all of them passed out in the trunk of the limo, their paws twitching like the hands of old men. They were the most beautiful animals I'd ever seen, too beautiful to be drugged like that and too calm to know their own rage.

6. "I Don't Wanna Fall in Love"

It was a strangely hot afternoon in the UP. The sky was a subjunctive blue. The sun saturated the air with orbs of merciful light. A bunch of us—me, the mixed-race poet and four ravishing nerds in a red convertible, if you can believe that shit—were driving up north, listening to Chris Isaak's "Wicked Game," our bodies flushed from hours of riding giant waves in wetsuits on Lake Superior that climbed into the sky like liquid cobras, splitting up into ephemeral armies of foam serpents. The waves reminded me of Katsushika Hokusai's tsunamis that my hapa mom had plastered all over the waiting room of her family therapy office: swelling walls of muted turquoise like volcanoes rising up from the ocean floor. In the car, as the wind pounded my sunburnt skin, I remembered thinking, *Today is perfect. I wish this moment was eternal. I wish it could live inside of me forever, immutable and crippling like a birth defect.* When we got hungry, we pulled off at some Podunk town that had a taco stand and sold pineapple tamales and cans of coconut juice. We licked the overflow on our sweaty cans, sitting at little wooden tables in the shade, lost in the hum of our bodies. The cook turned on his radio and played Mexican songs that sounded happy but were actually about heartache and poverty and longing. Lake Superior echoed in my ears back on the road even though the beach was twenty miles away now. The waves rang inside my head, pulverizing the stoic stones, polishing the air with karats of crushed sand. The lake seemed to murmur forever in a series of run-on sentences like a book of broken mantras. By the time we got back to Marquette, the waves were still colliding inside my head, racing up the beach to become foam and then atmosphere.

7. "Just Drive"

Ma is the problem. She doesn't use a belt when she hits me, she just goes for what's lying around and each relapse becomes a different stage production of hand puppets: Papermate pens, hairbrushes, tennis balls, extension cords, and pink plastic hangers. You'd be amazed how neutral objects can turn on you like a sharp corner. She isn't so bad when she's down on her luck and begging for a few bucks. Maybe, it's the humility and maybe, it's the pain. It's payday that really clobbers you like a construction boot in the ribs, sucking the quiet right out of your lungs. For a year now, I've been rolling up my shirtsleeves and saving up from my slowass dinner shifts. Last night, Ma dipped her hands into my shoebox again. She doesn't know I count the tally every night and then write down the total inside a borrowed physics textbook. I'm barely seventeen years old and most of my fam is still on the rez, so she's all I got besides Jimmy. She makes me feel lonely all the damn time. When I told her to lay off my box, she picked up the closest thing around, my trophy for perfect attendance at East Lansing High School (the only trophy I ever got) and chucked it in the mutating darkness. Right before it struck me in the face, there was a perfect sustain. Then, I saw lightning bolts inside my eyes. I knew right then I was done being her daughter. I called Jimmy while Ma was out at the Golden Phoenix Casino on the corner, a sharp corner actually, the kind that does the most damage when you run into it. Jimmy and I packed the few things worth taking and sped off in his hooptie to Detroit. Just for the hell of it, we drove through Lansing, which glowed like a busted-up, half-destroyed jukebox, the city lights groaning in the windows. When I smiled, my jaw rang. The pain felt like a single note deep in the marrow, humming like a tuning fork.

8. "Chinese Take Out"

A bachelor's degree in German from MSU and here I am getting paid nine bucks an hour to schlepp Papermate pens and school supplies from Birmingham to Livonia, Troy to Ypsi, Royal Oak to Canton for MOVERS AND SHAKERS Inc. Last Friday, I delivered a thousand canisters of old tennis balls to the Plymouth Home for Assisted Living. For their walkers, the orderly explained. Then, it was eight hundred boxes of white Reebok Fast Steps (all lefties) to a running store in Ann Arbor that took five hours because of a traffic jam on Jackson Road. After that, ten tiny mannequins sent from a blind woman living on the Euphrates to a little shop in Dearborn. The mannequins appeared in the windows a few days later wearing gold-plated saris and luminous shalwar kameez, the slender wrists covered in bangles like metallic worms. Two days ago, it was biblical popsicles to a Korean church in Detroit. And yesterday, on my last day, I delivered a thousand coconuts to an accountant's firm in Bloomfield Hills. After getting over his shock at seeing a thousand coconuts—it's an insane sight, I admit—he signed the form and shook his head. Now that the coconuts weren't mine anymore, I asked him what he was planning on doing with a thousand coconuts. He said he wasn't sure. He said maybe he'd drill a hole through one of the shells (three inches in diameter), put it in the microwave, and then fuck that big nut to his heart's content. He asked me if I wanted to watch. I folded the receipt, slipped it into his hand, and ran like hell. A few hours later, I realized I'd delivered the coconuts to the wrong place. People make their ones look like I's and their zeroes look like O's. My bad.

9. "Atrevida"

Roberto and Camila went off to school dressed in doll clothes that shrink in the sun, discolored and diminutive like nicknames. I told Camila she had until seven o'clock. If she was late again helping Samsona with her chores, she'd have to stay the night. The truth is, she *tries* to be late. We have our own problems and she's sick of moving the carro before night falls like a van of performing gitanos. You see, the streets fill up with patrol cars, borrachos, and injured cowboys. White men don't understand silence the way undocumented women do. The weekly move keeps us together, even if it's a pain sometimes. Usually, we roll down the windows, sip green coconuts bought from street vendors, and listen to mariachi as we pass Old Orchard or drive through Franklin Park, passing million-dollar homes with fountains and trimmed hedges and TV commercials strobing half-dressed bodies through open windows. I admire how clean white people's sidewalks are in the summer, the way they keep their homes so tidy, adorning porches with wicker baskets, little benches made of birch and banana wood, and pots of prickly pear cactus that come from the desert where my family grew up. I love the way Toledo smells at night, reminds me of tortillas de harina, the kind you buy back home when the roads shut down during traffic jams as old Mayan women sell you tamales de piña wrapped in corn husks that look like burlap ponchos. For fifty pesos, you can get a bag of twelve, piping hot, passed to you right through the open windows, fogging up the glass like new lovers. By the time you're done eating, the traffic has cleared and the bus is moving again. Es un milagro con que uno contaba.

I hope Camila comes back soon. Su ausencia me duele el estómago. I feel guilty rolling down the windows, it's just that the air smells like a valley in the Yucatan, like a clay oven in Campeche. If she was here, I'd tell her again about her primos that sleep in library stacks and study in bus depots back in México, dancing in outfits made from silver curtains and faded washcloths. Someday, I will tell Camila about my childhood all over again, about the only country that loves you like an only child even when you're all alone.

10. "Thirsty Wolverine Thot"

Right now, I need a break from A2. I can't listen to another convo about obscure garage bands with stupid garage band names selling out to greedy multinational corporations, the cultural appropriation of stinky white djembe drummers jamming on campus and white yuppies selling pineapple tamales and coconut water for ten bucks a pop on State Street, the cisgender rearview gaze of toxic masculinity, the plight of blue Bengali cubs in the illegal fur trade, and the slave trade of mannequin production on the Euphrates. Today, I'm writing a paper with tire tracks, break beats, and subwoofers. I'm blasting Black Pink in my Kona and driving solo with the windows down, coasting to Detroit with a j in my hand, ignoring omma's texts about picking up kimchi (*always* more kimchi) for the Baptist minister she's crushing on. I'm not in love with the D, I haven't even found a café there that serves legit oat milk. I prefer to study in hotel lobbies. I pretend I have a rich girlfriend. She's taking the elevator, I tell the concierge. She's like that, I say, swooping down from the penthouse in a flash of studied elegance. Oh, you're wearing my favorite dress, the only fabric that doesn't obscure you, I sigh. That imaginary space of mine in hotel lobbies, this interstitial life on the highway, the in-between world of M-10 and I-96, somewhere between the vinyl stores of Ann Arbor and the corroded Capitol of Lansing, between dog-eared theory books and late-night daydreams, is where I find my breath. This in-between is a timeless moment, a courageous flick of the wrist, a place to exhale in the trenches of old wars.

11. "Pause for a Comma"

I agreed to see Bikram only once. We would have one mango lassi together at a restaurant on Devon Street and then I would leave by myself in a taxi. That was the agreement. We met on Facebook, you see. Bikram was sweet and charming in the beginning. He sent me emails full of Punjabi proverbs and photoshopped pictures of the Golden Temple, Taxila, and the Mughal Gardens. He offered to pick me up at my job on Lakeshore Drive. I always declined. I felt safe inside a taxi. I *didn't* feel safe in a stranger's car, regardless of how pleasant he seemed in his emails. Besides, I've always had a love affair with taxis: the smell of old leather, a Cubs game muttering on the radio, the quietness of the backseat, other cars sliding between lanes on Lake Shore Drive like eels racing upstream, the intense beauty of Chicago's cityscape juxtaposed with the polluted majesty of Lake Michigan. I adored the space that taxis gave me to exist with my body, which is a simple pleasure for a brown woman in America. After Bikram and I finished our mango lassis, which were a bit salty for my tastes (but such is life), he insisted on giving me a ride home. I shook my head, tightened my sari, and stood firm. Taxis only, I said. I even paid the restaurant bill myself, so I didn't *owe* him anything. Bikram threw his napkin on the table. I tried to shake hands with him for the first and last time. He half-smiled, his bloodshot eyes gleaming with an intensity that terrified me. I said goodbye quickly and left the restaurant. A few blocks away, he called my name. I turned around, the voice inside my head screeching like a parakeet on fire. Bikram said he wanted to give me something before I disappeared forever and when I asked him what it was, he grabbed my arm and hurled me into the backseat of his white Cadillac. I tried unlocking the door, but it was child-safety locked, which explained his infantilization of me. The windows, the locks, everything was electric, everything under his command. I began to cry. He told me to *shut the fuck up.* He told me I was a whore for flaunting my beauty. He told me I was a bitch for rejecting his kindness. He told me he was one of the nice guys. He said desi sluts like me never gave men like him a chance. He said no one appreciated his kindness. When I woke up the next day, I was lying on my sofa, curled up like a little brown comma, covered with my sage throw I know for a fact I hadn't placed on myself. For a second, I thought I'd had a terrible nightmare until I stood up and felt sparks in the skin over my cheekbones. I walked into the bathroom and saw my body in the mirror covered in a camouflage of bruised skin and dried blood. I felt a dull flame between my legs. My jaw throbbed. My eyes were broken. I grabbed my phone and called papa-ji. When I got his voice mail, I slumped to the ground and sobbed. When he called back, he wasn't crying for the right reason.

12. "Broken Chords"

It was the hottest day of the summer and the worst possible day to play rugby. It felt like every Michigander was exhaling at the same time. When the light turned green, I hit the clutch and shifted into gear. Somewhere in the North End, I stopped at the crosswalk when I noticed a group of Korean uncles passing out blue popsicles from a church van, dishing them out to a throng of sun-broken pedestrians. People were going wild, screaming, *Me next, Me next,* pushing each other out of the way, hands in faces, elbows in diaphragms, wrists blocking an incessant scrum. When they were done, the church guys smiled long and hard at their flock. Finally, the wind caught one of the wrappers and sent it

through my window, the blue liquid oozing into my hand like a
sugary antifreeze:

Blue Raspberry-flavored Jesus-Loves-You Snack'n'Pops!

Salvation in every lick!

Repentance in every mouth!

I turned to a rabid white kid in the street with a large green
Mohawk and tight black pants. *Is this a joke?* I asked. He shook his
head and licked his fingers. *How's that thing taste,* I asked. *Like shit,*
he said, *but at least it's cold.* Just then, the cars behind me honked
their horns, echoing one after another like a Detroit arpeggio. I
crossed myself, turning left on the stickiest yellow light.

13. "Magnificent Loops"

After I cleaned up, I told her we were leaving. She didn't respond,
so I left her ass on that cliff and sped away. It wasn't until I got
sick of late-night traffic near Kalamazoo that I swerved onto
the shoulder and passed the gridlock on I-94. A state trooper
flashed his lights at me and I panicked, pounding the accelerator
with my Air Jordans. I could see my mug shot in all the papers,
a pink, zitty face trying to sneer with my eyes filled with abject
fear. I was afraid of prisons, cell bears, and hard-up street thugs
sodomizing me with unsharpened pencils and jump ropes just
because they could, afraid of my life spiraling out of control
before it began, my raw and misshaped body spooned to death
in the prison cafeteria, tattooed with safety pins dipped in blue
Papermate ink, and sacrificed in the laundry room by members
of the Aryan Nation who bludgeoned me with pillowcases filled
with Irish Spring soap. I could see everything when the state
trooper crept into my rearview mirror. In a few seconds, my life
would be on COPS. There would be Reggae music playing in

the background as officers dribbled my head against the hood, blurring my features and erasing my gender with one smudge. But then, a red Jetta stalled in the slow lane, making just enough room for me to barrel down the shoulder again. I did 110 mph with my nerves twisted and tangled into a reef knot, my head set on fire like a protesting monk. The last thing I remember after I crashed into that Neon was the driver's neck snapping like a chopstick.

14. "Speed"

You should have seen that white dude's face. We were racing down Jackson Road like idiots, the hoods of our cars humming elegiacally as yellow birch, black walnut, and redbud trees whizzed by like stage props in bad high school musicals. I pushed it to 103 mph, the formulae of my last physics exam swirling in my head: $P=(M)(V)$, $F=(M)(X)(A)$, $W- (F)(X)$. I zoomed through a yellow light. When I looked in my side mirror, there was gridlock forming around his car like fluorescent spokes in a girly BMX bike, the gridlock turning into a herringbone pattern all the way to the next intersection. Now, the road was just a silent film of sporadic headlights, whole rests, and empty streets. The truth is, some drivers can't handle speed—even fuel-injected, acid-cutting, chemical romance speed—because they don't understand that inertia has always been our first drug pusher. The first lover to tap our veins with a cold spoon.

HOW TO RUIN A PERFECTLY BAD DATE

You have four cardinal rules about first dates:

1. Avoid taking your date to that glassblowing studio up north. Otherwise, she might fall in love with KOTHAR, that smug glassblower with the pretty hapa skin, and leave you on the curb like yesterday's recycling (p. 21).

2. Suggest matter-of-factly that your heart is a SEMI-PERMEABLE MEMBRANE, a place where people's kindness, honesty, intelligence, self-awareness, and compassion can check in but never leave, like the Bates Motel (p. 177).

3. Strike a philosophical pose with your date by reminiscing about THE SHORT STORY YOU NEVER READ, which may or may not be a reference to the amnesia wand in *Men in Black*. If your date hates *Men in Black*, then it was definitely not a reference. If they love it, then it definitely was. Say you're open to interpretation (p. 273).

4. Make sure that the two of you go to a fancy French restaurant so that you can speak FRENCH VOWELS THAT MAKE YOU LOOK LIKE A GOLDFISH (p. 157).

TEN ZEN KOANS
TRANSLATED FROM JAPANESE, MANDARIN, WU, VIETNAMESE, THAI, FUJIAN, KOREAN, TIBETAN, HAKKA, JAVANESE, MIZO, NEPAL BHASA, KHASI, BURYAT, MALAY, PAIWAN, BURMESE, & OKINAWAN
BY JACKSON BLISS, PHD

I.[1]

II.[2]

III.[3]

IV.[4]

---

1 A second translation of this Zen Koan is:

2 Another possible translation of this koan, though certainly less elegant than Simmins's masterful 1995 volume, *Koans and Nothingness,* is:

3 An excellent critical analysis of this poem is available here:

4 There is not a perfect Burmese equivalent to this word in English. An alternative more colloquial translation might go something like   , though as Professor Zenzen Dogen at Tufts University, argues, "   "

V.[5]

VI.[6]

VII.[7]

VIII.[8]

---

is a more authentic translation because it preserves both the original meter, sound, and assonance of the Tibeto-Burmese word.

5 The *Anthology of*   provides a fascinating historical and cultural context for this koan.

6 Of course, this koan could also be thought of as "   " but this inelegant translation misses the homophonic harmony of "   " that lies somewhere between the word for air and the word for breath, which, unfortunately, does not exist in English.

7 Perhaps the single most difficult Wu concept to translate sociolinguistically, this word is often mistakenly translated as "   " by tone-deaf translators who are often less conversant with the etymological and morphological word play in this now defunct Zen expression for house cleaning, and by implication, infidelity, snoring, and skyjumping. Nevertheless, as Professor Vacío at Princeton University points out, even a literal translation of this word into "   " or "   " misses the obvious phonemic similarities to the original term, which is based less in the word "   " and more on the aspirated sound, "   ."

8 By far the longest and the most complex of the Japanese koans, this piece, according to the most recent archaeological evidence, dates this manuscript somewhere between the Jōmon and the Asuka periods, though some Buddhist scholars believe that the colloquial pictographs, especially those in the introductory and signature page, in addition to certain phraseology

IX.[9]

X.[10]

───

and idiomatic deviations after Volume III, place this epic koan in the
Azuchi-Momoyama period.

9 The authenticity of this Buryat koan, as delightful and succinct as it is, is
still considered spurious by The Academy of Buddhist Scholars, but I have
included it in this collection anyway, to give the reader a sense of the regional
variety at stake here.

10

READING PERSONALITY TEST

1. Jot down the first thing that comes to mind when you see the following words:
   - **A.** Corporate
   - **B.** Every
   - **C.** Day
   - **D.** America (p. 103)

2. You're at a party when you notice a Blackanese college student dressed up as Elvis Santa wearing fake Guccis. Your first instinct is to:
   - **A.** Call the fashion police
   - **B.** Smash his fake sunglasses against the crown of your head and shout, "I'm ON to you, motherfucker!" (p.93)
   - **C.** Headbutt him until he farts flowers
   - **D.** Sing "Love Me Tender" in Pig Latin

3. You arrive at a congested and chaotic intersection in the Loop when you realize the traffic light isn't working. This makes you wanna:
   - **A.** Eat an egg and mushroom crepe (p. 113)
   - **B.** Turn the heat up to 4
   - **C.** Shoot a Tik-Tok video of you tripping on your flip-flops
   - **D.** Moonwalk into the library

4. This test is just a big conspiracy to make you feel stupid. This makes you wanna:
   - **A.** Give up before it's too—oops, time's up. You failed again, bro (p. xxi)

BLUE IS THE LONELIEST NUMBER

1. Supermarket of Blue

It seems so easy now, the way their legs, forearms, and shoulder blades intersect like an intricate machine of human flesh, the engineering of their limbs working together flawlessly like the prize in a Kinder Surprise egg. Yumi looks down at her body and reimagines her lost visual field geometrically: the scalene triangles where her hands once were, the two rhombi where hamstring muscles once erupted from a canvas of taut skin, the rectangle below her collarbone where freckled breasts once looked like brown bullseyes. Now she sees raw, imagined color emanating from her solar plexus that bleeds into her bedroom in a supermarket of blue: the Mediterranean blue of Corfu beach houses, the supernal blue of Turkish mosque tiles, the haunting blue of Chagall's stained glass, the chilly blue of Scandinavian crystal, and the cratered indigo of old vases collected and stored on dusty window sills to play refraction games with the industrious sun.

Now, color is a conscious act of conception for Yumi. Even though she doesn't speak Spanish, she finds comfort in a story that Catalina, her best friend from grad school, told her once. In traditional Spanish, they don't say:

I had children.

They say:

Les di luz a mis hijos. I gave light to my children.

This is how Yumi feels right now. She is a mother conceiving children in the womb of color, their faces are midnight like the Blue Grotto of Capri, like the Blue Sapphire Gin in her glass, like the patrician blood in her mom's veins.

2. An Open Book

Yumi feels Renaldi's heartbeat through his abdomen. She likes resting her head on his stomach after catnaps, but not directly on her forehead scar. His stomach is another lesson she's learned: emotion and vitality can be translated into texture. The body isn't just a signifier of desire, identity, or vulnerability, but also a whole lexicon by which the human experience is communicated, a series of physical idioms that approximate mental states: pounding wrists, dry lips, apricot cheeks, quiet skin, and the dew point of palms. Lying on Renaldi's stomach, she has learned that his body is a language of his deepest and strongest feelings she has been teaching herself one lesson at a time. Her hands now read some of his emotions, but they often misread others.

—What's wrong? Yumi asks.

—Niente, Renaldi replies.

—No, it's not niente. It's something.

—Fine, it's something.

—You feel sad.

—I do?

—Yes, that's what it feels like.

—No.

—Then what?

—Today, I am shit. I want to feel joy but I don't.

—Can I touch your lips?

—Not now.

—Your arms?

—No.

—Kiss me at least.

—Turn on the light, Olfatto, I'm sick of darkness.

—Why?

—I want to see your face. I never get to look at it.

—Faces are misleading.

—So is darkness.

—Touch my face instead.

—I don't want to.

—Let me touch yours then.

—Don't.

—Renaldi, if I've upset you, I'm sorry. You can turn on the light if you want.

—What's the point?

—So you can see my face. Isn't that what you want?

—You can't see mine.

—Why does this bother you so much?

—Because I feel you love someone else.

—But we both do and that's okay.

3. The Compass of Green and Orange Blocks

With blindness comes creativity. Yumi must revisualize her lost world each and every day and her memory is hardly photographic. For this reason, she has decided that her mind is:

A coloring book for amnesiacs
A sketch pad of invisible art
A journal of air

Yumi is sleeping with ten different men every month even though it's always the same lover, even though it's always Renaldi, and this detail has made her blithe and kinky under the sheets. Each session of love is novel, refreshingly strange, and disobedient to memory. Each moment reminds her of Frankfurt: the metaphoricity of the bridges, the taste of country milk in the chocolate, and the Kinder Surprise diagrams in thirty (?) languages. Yumi loses herself to the gluttony of pleasure, to Renaldi's torso, their bodies forming a fresh relationship with nerve endings, fantasy worlds, and body heat. The story about the world she creates each day is lost when she sleeps because her memory is unfaithful to the material world, unfaithful to the rules of objective color. Renaldi is no longer the center of her life, he is just a glimmering moon of mysterious fluorescence in her planetarium. His smell and his voice both continue to mutate in her head according to the prisms of pheromones, the horoscopes of meter, and the oracles of skin texture.

4. Instruments of Music

Yumi waited until everything was perfectly still. She stepped off the curb with a walking cane and crossed the street in the eerie silence which Ann Arbor mornings are notorious for. She walked through open space that was once Lapsang Souchong Avenue until she stumbled inside a musty church off campus, smelling of stale incense and extinguished votives. She lay down on a pew like a late night drunk in a Leonard Cohen song and then waited until the choirmaster had finished talking about sforzandos and codas. In the cool and damp nave, a rapturous song emerged from the pulpit, voices rising up to the rafters, lingering like chords snagged in the air. After the ethereal cherubs sang the "Miserere Mei," Yumi saw cranes inside the church, hovering above the pulpit, graceful and wiry cranes like mere specks of melody rising above the choir stands and suspended in the smoke-filled air, congregating in the transept near the frosted stained glass and right above the apse, their long and thin wings fanning the tiny Jesus statue like slave girls of a Sultan. Now the world was a transmutation and music was a:

Mala of Japanese cranes lined up in a row, splitting up into threes and fours, mingling incestuously between bass and treble clefs.

Music was a migration of melody and birds were:

In the service of a higher power, delivering songs to the seven major tribes of the world. Cranes were simply musical notes with wings flying through the rafters of the human mind.

5. Glowing Open Book

It was after her world disintegrated into semi-pixelated darkness that she'd learned to identify the difference between a sigh of pathos, a sigh of unexpected pleasure, and a sigh of insecurity-masquerading-as-ennui in people. Blindness had become a monastery of synesthesia. Human skin was a half-open glowing book. At certain moments, she discovered that skin was a genius of sensation, recognizing the smallest nuance in pressure, warmth, or movement. In this temple of intangibility where her material ego was slowly plucked like millipede legs, Yumi let go of her attachment to Renaldi's beauty (which was hard at first, dude was fucking hot). The problem with making love had always been that it had to end at some point. It began with foreplay, circling fingertips grazing erogenous hairpin curves, smooth palms gliding down thighs sweet and smooth like rice candy, it continued with their Mesozoic engineering, inciting mobs of blood cells to sprint through leg capillaries as her clit swelled and her longing tidalwaved through her bones, as a hot and burning sensation rioted through her skin, the circumference of her pleasure expanding past the suburbs of functionality, the pleasure so throbbing and so expansive she couldn't contain it anymore. When they made love now, her pleasure wasn't functional, it wasn't in the service of some mythical idea, it wasn't stumbled-upon pleasure, it was rebellious pleasure, the pleasure of the sodomitical mother, the revolution against functionality where bodies expressed affection for each other, using fingers, lips, and tongues as interpreters of unvocalized desire.

6. The Triumphant Bugle

—Okay, put your hands here, he said.

—Now what? she asked.

—Now, pick the pencil.

She scowled. —Renaldi, you're trying to trick me. You've got three Bic mechanical pencils and . . . one gel roller. And this is a Sharpie, so there's *three* pencils.

—Bene. That was a gift.

—Make it harder.

—Okay. Which is grapefruit and which orange?

Yumi touched each fruit with her hands and inhaled. —Um, *this* is the grapefruit. No, wait, *this* is the grapefruit. You can tell by the smell.

—If you say so.

—Am I right?

—Sì, Olfatto.

—Cool. Now can we go underneath the sink? I can never tell the difference between fabric softener and detergent.

7. Trumpet-Playing Angels

Yumi moved her hands across the walls of her craftsmen house in Kerrytown, noticing the bumpy texture in the paint. There were thousands of fragmented Braille plot twists, histories, and myths all pressed into the hard surface of her drywall like a secret library hiding within the walls. She used to love these walls back when she could distinguish between avocado and shamrock green, but the slow deterioration of her vision, what she once ignorantly referred to as the death sentence of material color, also meant a loss of kitsch, especially during her daily walks to the Old West Side and back. To her this meant the erasure of:

1. Bubblegum pink button-downs on young alcoholics detoxing on green coconuts
2. Nike swooshes brandished on insecure men
3. Overplucked black eyebrow worms
4. Midwestern women with brassy blond dye jobs driving in SUVs
5. Tony-the-Tiger-Princeton-Orange gowns and dirty U of M baseball caps
6. Obese Trump supporters driving black hummers down Liberty with NRA and "Fuck Your Feelings" bumper stickers
7. Violin players busking on the corner like desolate angels
8. Dancers (or Were They Priests?)

As her world faded from her collective mind, her fingers were discovering an ancient language of texture for the first time. Even six months ago, it was impossible. Reading used to be the prerogative of her eyes. She only used her fingers to turn pages, accepting their humble role as servants of her visual field, as common messengers of language, but then one day her soft fingers were expected to flesh out a coherent narrative from a battlefield of paint smudges and goose bumps. Her untrained fingers didn't know how to sniff out secret objects or material romance. They weren't drug dogs, for god's sakes! Now, texture was an alphabet, bumps were a foreign language, and reading had become an abacus of lost words slowly adding up a lexicon inside her head. Yumi's fingertips glided over the smooth, nippy windowpanes, past the closed Kawai piano that no longer sang the notes of Gershwin or Rachmaninoff until she came to the tape deck in her fancy stereo console. She wanted to tape herself so later on, she could listen to her voice and hear the inflection of the viewer, to remember what it felt like to turn each day into a graphic novella of nothingness, or protest her life by sleeping in.

9. The Guitar and the Violin

Their lovemaking got lost in the finitude of desire, in the sticky confusion of their newly divorced worlds, and in the obsolescence of the body's designs. She worried that they would never learn to make love the way they once did when she could take her eyesight for granted. Love became a palpitating vulnerability she'd grown to hate more than solitude, more than Dr. Peterson's palpable sadness after he'd given her the bad news, and more than the smog of brooding men in every café in

A2. Yumi hated this more than anything and now she feared that the same thing was happening to her relationship with Rinaldi: when straight lovers transmogrified into time-released strangers, stuck in that space where men buttoned up striped oxfords and women zipped up jean skirts in silent urgency, where former lovers, released from their indentured appetites stopped looking at each other with the same glow anymore, where hands that once wrote love letters on the hills of the back and the shoreline of the stomach disappeared from the compass of sexuality, their new boundaries drawn up with blunt elbows, staggered dinner schedules, and prolonged absence. Personal space was the way lovers spoke in the register of separation and separation was the way lovers gave birth to division, their method for breastfeeding their own dissolution as a couple. Yumi's body understood everything in real time, her imagination in erotic time, and her mind in moral time. She felt jetlagged traveling between her own time zones.

10. The Cities Down Below

—Yumi, which is peach, which is tangerine, and which apricot?

—That's easy. *This* is the tangerine . . . that's the peach . . . and *this* is the apricot. The fuzz is a dead giveaway.

—Scusa, ma, that's not right. The first is apricot and the third is tangerine.

—Motherfucker goddammit shit. Okay, next!

—Which one is apple and which potato?

—Okay, bring them closer . . . lower. Okay, your left hand is the potato? Let me smell your right hand. Oh, that's the apple. I can smell the fructose.

—Brava, brava! From now on, I call you Olfatto.

—I don't like that. It sounds like "Old Fat." It's a terrible nickname.

—It just means the nose is growing up.

11. Cupped Hands

God, her eyesight was starting to fade. Walking through her apartment was like wandering through a half-lit cave. Yumi went into the kitchen and opened up the miscellaneous drawer. She formed a claw with her hand and let it sink into the landfill until her nails touched the cherry wood bottom. With a Maglite, she navigated through:

> Grocery receipts, Peace Rally flyers, Kodaks of children hanging from monkey bars, a tiny bag of Kinder Surprise eggs, and thumbtacks jabbing her fingers like miniature fencers ("En garde!" they shouted)

Her delicate fingers slid through:

> An instruction manual for a lost blender, business cards for upstart acupuncture therapists and chiropractors

Her soft, elegant, tiny little hands pushed through:

> A box of expensive German watercolors, a ticket stub from the *Musei Vaticani*, the last letter her daughter had ever written her, a blue jelly pen filled with glittering stars that crashed into each other like celestial prophecies

She dug her hands into:

> A key to a lost armoire from the '83 fire, boxes of
> chipped birthday candles, a series of sunset photos in
> Alaska, brown shoe polish, speckled origami paper,
> and postcards from Nagoya, Frankfurt, Dubrovnik,
> Tokyo, Paris, the Pike Street Market, Berlin, Florence,
> and the Japanese Garden of Portland, all shackled by
> rubber bands.

Finally, she retracted her arm like a 50-cent crane and held two blank cassettes. It seemed hard to believe that space—in this case, her craftsman house—could be converted into language, but she didn't have another idea and time was running out. She felt like she was competing against the sunset.

12. Sideways Ballerina

In the Ashram of Stolen Light, Yumi learned that the human world was a perishable playbook of the universe, a perfect law of entropy and cosmic degeneration. Somehow, her eyes were part of that cosmic degeneration. She was once double-knotted to Renaldi's body, his deep-set eyes, his copper-olive skin, his Roman nose, and his throwing-knife jaw line, but now she was losing her grip on the dictatorship of archetypes. She knew that once she went blind, a part of her would die. That wasn't ableist melodrama, just the delayed acknowledgement that the way she'd defined herself growing up as someone who understood reality with her eyes, was going to radically change in the next couple years. Soon, she'd have to recreate reality however she could. She'd have to pretend she was a ballerina, always airborne, always defying gravitational theory, always defying the functionality of objects. She'd have to pretend Renaldi was always staring at her, even when he was playing eye-ballet with some young tart at the Kerrytown Farmers Market, even when he was plotting to steal her favorite print (*I and the Village*) from her living room, or drive his Alfa Romeo off a cliff into Lake Michigan after she'd asked him if she was beautiful a hundred times and then cried when he stopped answering.

13. Lemon Moon

In the darkness:

—Renaldi, I'm not putting on that stupid scarf! It's like 90° outside!

—Yumi, stop cheating. You peek.

—I literally *can't* cheat.

—Yes, you can. You still see during the day. And during the night with the fuzz. You said so.

—No.

—How did you know there was a full moon last night?

—Okay, fine.

—Just put it on, per piacere. Does this hurt?

—Not as much I wish it did.

—Bene. Now, which is peach and which apricot?

—Um, *this* is the peach.

—If you say so.

—Well, *is* it or *isn't* it?

Renaldi made a buzzer sound with his voice.

—Argh. I can't do this!

—Sì, you can. Just keep trying.

—Fine. *This* is the peach.

—No, those all apricots. *This* is Mrs. Peach.

—Kuso! It feels like a goddamn apricot to me.

—Yes, but it's not.

—This is impossible, Renaldi. I'll never learn how to do this!

—No, Yumi, not impossible. Noses can be fingers and fingers can be eyes.

Yumi tried her hardest to hold back her tears. Renaldi pulled her against him and held her until her breathing stabilized. He smelled like home, filling her lungs with joy, comfort, and immense sadness now.

14. Menorah

First Candle: Yumi was relieved to find out that Budget Rent-a-Car didn't have a database of people going blind because she would have been shit out of luck. Two hours later, she was sitting at Cannon Beach. Yumi pulled out old watercolors from another lifetime and painted the Oregon coast in slow strokes that resembled koi circles. She painted with a singular focus that came from the ardent understanding of imminent loss. She knew the visual world would slowly disappear from her life, so she was obsessed with capturing Haystack Rock (that massive Sumo Wrestler in the middle of the shoreline), Yumi's hands moving in sync to the errant choreography of pink kites bursting in broken orbits, looping in frenetic figure eights in the patchwork summer sky. Yumi felt lost in her art, lost in the pristine sand and the smell of cold kelp, and lost in the fading sunlight, which felt more and more personal each day. The waves crashing on the shoreline made her ears ring, the night transforming the horizon into a stained-glass mosaic: lightning bolts splintered the cobalt sky into gradient shards, storm clouds rolled towards the shoreline carrying the apocalypse in their folds.

Second Candle: Yumi had loved Germany the way only a Nisei could, not for its language (nicht so recht), but for its chocolate hazelnut pastries, its green spaces, its punctual trains, and the cleanliness and order of its cities that were both functional and efficient. She especially loved Frankfurt: the way its bridges would lift her small body into the foggy morning air towards medieval Römerberg, Sachsenhausen, and the Ziel Shopping district. She loved watching geese strut on the riverbank like disco dancers. She loved the sound of her feet tapping on the steel planks, clip-clopping on arched roman cobblestone walkways, and clicking on smoothly paved cement, from one side of The River Main to another. Yumi even loved the symbolism of Frankfurt's bridges: a man-made structure reconnecting fragmented pieces of land, a reunion of sexual geography, a metaphor of sex and language, and the intercourse of divided space overcoming the same chasm through movement. She loved the city for its mathematical and spatial proportions. She'd loved it for its emotional registry too. After all, she'd fallen in love with a boy there once who'd looked like a young Brahms. She discovered the hidden courage in that city to reach out to the other side and fall in love for the first time with Jonas, a grad student at Goethe University who used to buy her milk candy and sketch her face as she slept, always drunk on art theory, charcoal portraits, and Grauburgunder.

Third Candle: Yumi took her change, shoved it in her purse, and held the ticket up to the light: JAPANESE GARDEN OF PORTLAND. After wandering through the Natural Garden and the Tea Garden—the sign said closed, but she didn't care—Yumi stopped at the Sand and Stone Garden, trying to remember the fable of the Buddha and the six cubs. What was it exactly? The Buddha had starved in protest of the dying cubs? Or had he offered up his body as food to the cubs? She could never get it straight. After admiring the Shirakawa sand in the garden that was carefully raked into little circles, Yumi arrived at the Pond Garden where she gazed at the murky water as chubby koi swam in complex polygons. There was something so placid, aristocratic, and pointless about their trajectories as their paths crisscrossed, mouths opening and closing, reciting underwater mantras, tails and scales rubbing against each other, each koi circling around, lost in a constant sequence of loops, the water sutra falling from their mouths with every spiral, their words spoken in air bubbles that sank to the bottom of the pond. Yumi knew this was probably the last time she would see these fish lost in perpetual devotion and gliding through the reflection of the changing color of the sky. The lump in her throat felt like a giant ball of phlegm.

Fourth Candle: When she was studying art history at Notre Dame as an undergrad, Yumi wanted to fall in love because nothing was more romantic, suicidal, flawed, or emo than the pain that came after unrequited love, but she had to settle for drunken hookups to avoid appearing clingy (or pretending she wanted to get married, just to avoid getting slut-shamed). After she left Germany with Jonas's conveniently timed, crumpled breakup letter in her satchel, she returned to Ann Arbor and finished her dissertation, sublimating her grief into her writing until she'd found an academic publisher before she'd even done her thesis defense. To everyone's surprise, she became an assistant professor at the same school where she'd gotten her PhD, which never happened (her two publishing contracts with Oxford University and Wayne State University Press for two separate monographs definitely didn't hurt). During the rainy winter nights of her last year in grad school, she searched for the perfect glass of Grauburgunder at Spencer to cure her weltschmerz for the expatriate-researcher life that was no longer hers, for a world that had never been hers. And now at the twilight of her senses, Yumi had become obsessed with seeing a perfect Michigan sunset: cloudy and restrained one moment, explosive and ineffable the next. They reminded her that light was transitory, always stolen from the day, always borrowed from the night, always palmed from the sun. Watching sunsets was like witnessing the planet hurl a discus of dazzling energy into the sea, incanting the darkness to snuff out the blaze. Yumi's vision, however, would never come back. It was a fact she couldn't accept. During her trip to Seattle, she'd spent a whole hour looking at Mt. Rainier—that great riddle of mass hunched in the sky—and then back again at the sound where ferries floated toward Vashon, Camano, and Bainbridge Islands. The sun's neon circumference sank in a great sizzle. In another life where she could see perfectly and where she'd applied to tenure-track jobs even in parts of the country she didn't want to live in, like in the Pacific Northwest, Seattle could have been her home. Counterfactual love stories always hit her the hardest because they disobeyed every rule she'd fought so hard for. Yumi felt haunted by other versions of herself. In other timelines, she was allowed to see mountain tops each night, fall in love with strangers on a ferry, go on dates in Lower Queen Anne, and spend hours gazing at each other's naked and unfamiliar bodies, taking their lives for granted, waking up every morning and seeing each other half-dressed, almost divine in the light's refraction, almost disassembled in the sleep.

Fifth Candle: Some things were faithful to memory, even when a tad bit blurry. Saturday afternoons at the Pike Street Market, for example. Yumi knew she could count on the dragoons of Chinese American women selling tight bouquet bundles and feast on free samples of homemade jellies and nut butters, she knew there would always be stands selling hand-made straw hats, carved wooden figures, essential oils, and fake Indian incense, water colors a hundred times better than her own, black and white photos of Mt. Rainier, German, Arabic, and Taiwanese newspapers, small soccer fields of fresh glistening vegetables, and cinnamon and sugar donuts made right in front of your eyes—conveyor belt and all. She remembered the first time she saw a king salmon flying through the air, the Pike Street Fish Boys dressed in orange rubber jumpsuits, singing back customer orders in their two-second musical. She remembered the first time she'd seen Renaldi here on a campus visit. His face was covered in salt and pepper stubble, a nose like an exiled emperor, lashes that were arresting, lips so fresh and captivating they seemed to be bleeding, and that face, that unlawfully beautiful and Mediterranean face, staring at her in the eternal pause of physical attraction, devouring her fear, standing there in his stinky, carrot-colored galoshes, his wet green eyes like lichen, his smile sparkling through her body. He was a Florentine prince standing in a cemetery of dead fish. It didn't matter that her memory was now having a love affair with the psychedelic stanzas of old age. She still remembered that moment in luscious detail. It was the moment she'd finally let go of the affair her ex-husband had been having with a jazz singer he'd met at a festival in Toronto. It was the moment she'd finally let go of the self-hatred she'd been lugging around like a flat-tired RV. The simplicity and the lightness she'd felt when Renaldi smiled at her that day became a form of liberation. She and Renaldi exchanged phone numbers in a dazed little whisper, their hands grazing each other in front of petrified Alaskan king crab and the o faces of rainbow trout. After she'd returned to A2, she texted him as she took a bath and he sent her a video of him playing guitar for a sleeping street dog. That was how the crush became the wound.

Sixth Candle: She looked up, the lights of Paris burning faintly through the paranormal haze enshrining Sacré Coeur. Every time a front door opened, she heard French hymns. Yumi knew all about Sacred Heart. Ms. Fitzgerald, her frumpy Pope-loving theology teacher at her Catholic prep school, would go on and on about all the great saints and the *devilish saboteurs* arriving on the historic steps of the Sacred Heart: Saint Denis, Saint Vincent de Paul, and Jeanne D'arc. Don't forget Saint Francis Xavier and Saint Ignatius Loyola, those *cunning men who founded that whole Society of Jesus thing in 1534, thereby splitting the Church Triumphant.* Yumi also knew the hidden part of church history Ms. Fitzgerald had deliberately omitted: a Benedictine Abbey torn apart by the French Revolution, the sisters of perpetual devotion, revered, canonized, and then guillotined all in the same year. And the face, yes, the *face* on the front of the basilica, two eyes below the right and left domes, the three Romano-Byzantine archways resembling nostrils, the steps like a long accordion tongue swallowing worshippers and tourists indiscriminately. Sacred Heart was actually Sacred Face. From a nearby bench, Yumi closed her eyes and tried to make out the hymns as the front doors opened and closed, filtering out the sounds of yelling American and Australian teenagers, the droning voice of a Chinese tour guide, and the sounds of cameras clicking. Yumi tried to hear the fluttering of little birds in the nave. She imagined them circling her head like messengers of forgotten melody, a gold scroll hanging from their jagged talons. She knew the birds of forgotten song had escaped the vestibule and soared outside in the Parisian twilight when she heard these words sung by abandoned angels:

> *Seigneur Jésus, ton sang versé nous purifie, Kyrie Eleison.*
> *O Christ, ta mort nous rend la vie, Christe Eleison.*
> *Seigneur Jésus, ton amour est—*

Yumi opened her eyes. In the distance, Paris floated in ether like a city in the clouds, like a fugue of perpetual devotion inside her head.

Seventh Candle: It had been seven years since she'd been back to the Art Institute of Chicago and feasted her eyes on blue stained glass. Yumi thought of that iconic scene in *Ferris Bueller's Day Off* where Matthew Broderick and Mia Sara kissed to the instrumentalized version of The Smiths' "Please, Please, Please Let Me Get What I Want" that she used to be so obsessed with in high school and then again in grad school. Yumi knew Chagall's *America Windows* intimately. As an obsessive, atheistic, and lonely college student studying art history and exploring her sexuality, she'd spent countless Saturdays taking day trips to Chicago to bask in the crisp blue sunlight. After all, it was the only work of stained glass she'd ever seen that touched her as a young woman, the only piece of glass that merited so much infatuation for so many unknowable details, and the only work of art that made her cold enough to put on a cardigan every time she looked at it. In her alternative music loving days in Chicago, she'd been fascinated, consumed really, with the way Chagall's blue glass was a deep shivering blue, if blue could be deep and shivering. In college, as boyfriends became fleeting cautionary tales or half-broken springboards to womanhood, Yumi focused her attention on the figures themselves in the mosaic every time she took a train from South Bend to Chicago: angels harking, scenes of Jewish families praying (signifying her relapsed Catholicism), a man falling from the sky (a signifier of college boys she'd dropped from the celestial sphere for loving DuChamp toilets, post-structuralism sound bites, or Cézanne still-lifes). The mosaic was plagued by portraits of couples in every stage of love and detonation, her greatest hope and failure in her 20s until she'd caught Jonas drawing her in Café Schwarz. After living in Ann Arbor for twenty-five years, after one failed marriage with a cello-playing gigolo, and after the birth of an impressionable daughter who'd moved in with the first man she'd fucked, this time Yumi looked at Chagall's blue windows with a robust history of trauma and heartache. She barely noticed the blocks of blue space and cratered indigo, the incomplete menorah, the dancers (or were they priests?) standing together, the trumpet-playing angel, the man falling from the geometric sky, the guitar and violin, the miniature models of urban American life spawning across all three windows, the glowing open book, the ballerina in profile, or the man surrounded by a compass of orange and green blocks. No, this time, all of Yumi's attention was focused on the raspberry dove fluttering its wings, flying to the glowing citric moon cradled by a pair of calloused, cupped hands. Yumi sat transfixed, unaware that her own hands were unbuttoning her cardigan as a Finnish tour group perched around her like a silent flock. She knew that the laws of fluid dynamics prevented

Chagall's dove from flying to the stratosphere where the air thinned and mountains converged. Only artists, mirrors, and birds—messengers of color, duality, and song—could ignore the laws of gravity.

15. In the Geometric Sky

In her spacious first-class seat (because why the hell not?), Yumi read her list over again, ignoring all the things she'd circled, crossed out, circled again, crossed out a second time, and then circled a third. Compulsion was an exhausting form of subtraction of the self. Her eyes felt dry, her contacts stuck to her eyeballs, gritty and sandy, and the bruise on her forehead, the one shaped like a blood lotus, was still sensitive to the touch. At least it was healing. When the stocky flight attendant asked Yumi if she wanted polenta with turkey sausage or vegetarian pasta with grilled asparagus, Yumi asked for two vegetarian pastas. The flight attendant raised her eyebrows and replied, *Okay, love.* Chicago was only nine hours away from London, where she'd flown for a long weekend to see the Rosetta Stone (and also witness the insatiable appetite of the British empire) one last time. Yumi shrugged her shoulders and looked down at her list.

Things I Need to See One Last Time before
the World Goes Dark

- ~~Children playing~~
- ~~Lunar Equinox~~
- ~~Live sex show~~
- ~~British Museum, Shoreditch, Notting Hill,~~
  ~~& Piccadilly Circus~~

- Chagall's *America Windows*
- Sacré Coeur.
- Pike Street Market in the springtime and Mt. Rainier
- 1,000 Ann Arbor sunsets
- Portland Japanese garden
- Frankfurt bridges
- Oregon Coast

16. The Falling (Wo)man

Yumi sat in a hospital chair, fidgeting her toes and flipping through old copies of *National Geographic* while CNN played in a loop on TV and news bytes and stock figures raced by on the chyron. She glanced at pictures of the Amazon rainforest but was too nervous to read about Runa culture in the Quichua community. All she could think of was:

> Her eyes, burning to death like old stars
> Her mom, who'd lost her vision in one eye by the age of
>   forty-five
> The Chagall print hanging in her avocado-colored
>   living room.

Yumi felt like Dr. Peterson had her whole life in his cupped and skilled hands. Technically, he was just an interpreter of her biology, helping her decode her own genetic history, but she liked to think he had special powers to rescue her from her gene pool.

Dr. Peterson came out dressed in grey wool pants, a physician's coat, green plaid button-down, grey tie, and grey plastic frames. His hair was sculpted into a silver wave. —Yumi? Come with me. Let's talk.

She followed him into the consultation room and sat down.

Dr. Peterson unbuttoned his physician's coat, took a deep breath, and exhaled. He looked in her eyes and pursed his lips, the sadness already leaking into his face.

Yumi tapped her feet and exhaled. —Well? she asked.

—Yumi, every test so far has come out the same.

—So, what's happening to me?

—You have an aggressive case of exterior retinal dystrophy.

Yumi understood medical jargon, but she waited for Dr. Peterson to rephrase the verdict. Only when something was committed to language did she accept it. It was one of her academic weaknesses.

—You're going blind, Yumi.

—Oh my god.

—Yumi.

—Oh my god. I've got my mom's eyes. All her Czech in-laws have issues with their vision.

—Yes, it's genetic, if that's what you mean.

—How can this be happening?

—This is—

—Why do I have *her* eyes?

—This is the address of a support group in Ypsi.

—Why can't I have my otōchan's eyes?

—Yumi.

—I'm a fucking art history scholar for fuck's sake!

—I *know* this has got to be difficult.

—You can't even imagine.

—You're right, of course, I can't, but I'll do everything I can to help.

Yumi's eyes welled up. Her life had been falling apart for the past three months, but now her body had joined the sedition: her ex-husband had just moved in with a twenty-seven-year-old scat singer from Royal Oak, only two students passed their Russian Constructivism midterms before she'd devised an insane curve to rescue half the students, and Yumi missed her daughter terribly. But these things seemed abstract now, like reading a fairytale about the future. She had no idea how she was going to live without light or color, alienated from her visual field, and forced to live without her academic livelihood. How could anyone expect her to put on a brave face while she slowly lost her grip on the material world, left to forage on sounds and textures? Yumi thought of her white mom who had accidentally taken her career from her, which was the only thing she had right now. Her white mom had destroyed every color she'd worked so hard to understand, every color she'd devoted her life to growing up.

Yumi looked at Dr. Peterson, whose eyes were filled with a sad, hopeless determination. —She's stolen my life from me, she said.

—Yumi, he said, you still have your life. It will always be yours.

—No, it was never mine. Don't you see? I was basically renting my life.

Dr. Peterson opened his mouth to comfort her, but Yumi stood up and ran outside, the mist in the crisp air creating a vaporous halo in the grey afternoon sky. In the parking lot, her chest began contracting as she sobbed, tears shooting down her cheek bones like the tails of comets, chiseling contour lines into her trembling skin. Her eyes became long streaks of mercury, transforming into the spells of wrathful gods. She wiped her eyes with her shaking hands and stumbled to her half-paid Volvo. In the driver's seat, she gripped the steering wheel with both hands and then slammed her forehead into the horn and screamed until her furious duet with her car became an unbearable indictment of the living and the lost.

YOU HAD A DREAM ONCE THAT YOU WERE SITTING AT A CAFÉ IN ST GERMAIN-DES-PRÉS, VORACIOUSLY READING A COLLECTION OF EXPERIMENTAL SHORT STORIES CALLED *META-COUNTERFACTUAL LOVE STORIES & OTHER META-EXPERIMENTS*, AND IN THIS DREAM, YOU SPOKE FRENCH WITH EFFORTLESS FLUENCY AND WHEN THE WAITER ASKED YOU WHAT YOU WERE READING (BECAUSE, YOU KNOW, FRENCH WAITERS ARE NOTORIOUSLY NOSEY), T'AS DIT:

1. « RIEN DE SPÉCIAL, JUSTE QUARANTE CHANSONS POUR LE PLACARD À CHAUSSURES» (p. 43).

2. «LES CODES SECRETS» (p. 35).

3. «LE BLEU EST LE CHIFFRE LE PLUS SOLITAIRE» (p. 65).

4. «L'EXAMEN D'ENTRÉE À MON COEUR» (p. 149).

HOW NOT TO FIND LOVE WITH YOUR FAKEASS GUCCIS

Even though your fakeass Guccis make you feel like some douchebag English major drunk on modernism, with the right flirty eyes, intensity, and savoir-faire, your fakeass Guccis can be magnetic. You've explained this to your little brother Dikembe like a *million* times. When you're an attractive mixed-race Asian/Blasian dude and you wear black rectangular plastic frames, the ones with the temples that flare behind your earlobes, white college students will lit talk to you out of the blue, practically begging for your approval, asking you about your playlists, asking you how to roll joints, asking you to drink Darjeeling tea with them inside hotel atria with Vivaldi playing in the background (and you fucking hate Vivaldi more than scorched-earth Bernie bros). They might drag you to line-breaking poetry readings at vintage-style apartments in Edgewater or invite you to badly-lit pop smut exhibitions in unheated warehouses in the West Loop with a Detroit DJ spinning house music no one has ever heard before. They might talk with you at a South Loop café about Sophocles, Baldwin, and Derrida in front of bay windows as the Chicago wind bitch-slaps the glass. Because the bar is so low with basic straight dudes and because you actually wear stylish glasses, dress like a GQ editor, and talk about the "morphology of desire," (a term you lit just wrote down for your brother to mumble out loud), people may find him urbane, original, and redemptive for a split second—until he opens his dirty mouth. You'll learn real quick, you explain, that white people use people of color to feel better about themselves, more out of expediency and insecurity than prejudice. It still feels bad either way. If your stars are misaligned, there might even be snide dialogue at an expensive café in Wicker Park, or a pretentious grad student party in Evanston, or some flirty repartee in the hallway, all of which will destroy your soul because you don't understand what's going on and you don't want to. That pain will be all your fault, no one else's, but at least you'll feel alive for a few seconds in your grief.

That was your life in your early twenties, back when indie music meant garage and every conversation on campus became a mini-Ted lecture on Blackness and/or mixed-race identity. But you're too old for this shit now and you need the infinite possibility of love in your relationships because that's just how you roll. Your younger brother, on the other hand, just wants help picking up girls, which you refuse, but you will help him become an evolved human being who can talk to other human beings, nothing else. Besides, you don't want him getting advice from misogynistic Pick-up Artist websites. You oblige him because you're sick, bed-ridden, and mildly compassionate and you know someone needs to fill his vacuum of knowledge. Your brother is *almost* like you, except lazier, stupider, and less inquisitive about people. He doesn't want to write the *Guide to Falling in Love with Evolved Human Beings* the way you did, he just wants to *glance* at it, maybe underline a few passages to prove he's done his homework. He's the worst kind of student of all, the kind of undergrad you routinely failed in grad school for having such low expectations of himself due to male and class privilege. You just returned from volunteering in Malaysia where you fell in love with a Balinese woman who ignored you for six months because of your Blasian blood, which she said wasn't personal (just structural, right?). Now, you're recovering from an unglamorously acute case of amoebic dysentery and a strange (terrible) bindi pimple, so you're hanging out at your parents' house for the next month until you feel healthy again. You're what they call a captive sensei. You don't even like your brother sometimes, you just wanna shut him up and prevent him from treating people (or sex) like a game. You desperately need some peace and quiet, so you agree to help him evolve, which is too much work.

Anyway, you continue, there are three cardinal rules for connecting with people.

The Three Cardinal Rules

The first rule: you need to *understand* human beings, which is so much work. Understanding people with different gender, sexual, cultural, class, and/or racial identities is even more work. The important thing is that you do it by asking questions and by listening. And since your little brother is an idiot and an otaku and a bad subject, his best bet is to ask a lot of questions. It might be his only chance to evolve since his work ethic is shitty. This will also make people feel important and he might just learn something about a world he's too lazy to understand.

The second cardinal rule: you need to buy fake prescription glasses. They'll make you look intellectual and also hide zits, fine lines, and worry bags underneath your eyes. Everything else is optional.

The third cardinal rule: kickass humans won't fall for *any* of these rules, which is how you'll know you've found the right person. And in case you're still curious (lazy), here's what you should already know but don't because you're fucking clueless and probably sexist.

The Six Small Rules

1. In your spare time, consider reading. If you can't kick the habit of being a consummate lazyass (or you realize you have a legit learning disability that you're too lazy to address), at least learn to disagree with everyone. In that case, don't worry about reading novels or purchasing new albums since you're too unmotivated to understand them. Just *knowing* about them makes you smart, in a way. Compile lists of books, influential thinkers, cult albums, and pop culture references. Spend the next month checking out dead corporate publishing companies like Borders and Warner Books (RIP) before studying Indiebound and Metacritic. If you're pressed for time, Google "mansplaining," "metoo," and "get off my TERF, man!". If you're at a café in Logan Square or Andersonville or the South Loop or Evanston and a person brings up a book you've never heard of (which will be always, in your case), just roll your eyes and tell them you feel like throwing up. They will either defend themselves by laying out the entire book for you in three easily digestible sentences (an intellectual parry), or they will find your candor charming and your negativity challenging, they might even laugh with you (which is a tiny détente). But like you'd know the difference, you goddamn poser. And by the way, just in case it's not obvious by now, positive consent for EVERYTHING is the law of the land until told otherwise (and even then, remember that it can be revoked at any time), so respect people's boundaries and never

creep on them, or you'll end up in the Shitty Media Men folder in your 20s and totally deserve it.

2. If you figure out how to pretend-play the electric guitar, write puzzling verse, or construct works of industrial art out of rusty bicycles and insulation tubes that you found in some back alley, these skills might help you stand out a tiny bit. Just don't exploit that shit! Act like you're too busy to spend time with anyone, which isn't hard with smartphones, and before you know it, you'll be completely and absolutely alone. Congrats! If you're going for that Kanye dragon energy bullshit, I guess you could act like you're too busy for the world. I mean, that might increase your appeal to some deranged lunatic, especially if you told a classmate you're an artist and talked about your so-called vocation in a vague and imprecise way. You could even complain that you're sick of explaining *what art is to people who don't get what art is*, even if they're artists themselves. They'll be intrigued/annoyed/pissed off by your dismissiveness, and you'll have time to think of an answer of why you're such a miserable human being. When all else fails, you could always use the antithesis cop-out by claiming that "art is the opposite of whatever you think it is," whatever the hell that means.

3. Avoid looking directly at people. Instead, watch their reflection in the mirror. Or if you're on the El, look out the window. When they try to look at you in reflection, look at their profile. This will help destabilize your male gaze and also prevent you from victimizing people when you stare too long and make them feel self-conscious.

4. Master the art of *SheisterWissen* too. Liberals will think you're smart as long as you embrace doctrinal simplicity, context, data, nuance, the art of critique, and paradoxically, the church

of permanent wokeness. Conservatives will think you're smart as long as you embrace doctrinal simplicity, moral absolutism, broad-brush strokes (like this paragraph), conspiracy theories, legalism, nationalist rhetoric, and the public performance of religiosity, just like liberals with wokeness. One-liners work on both parties, by the way, because wit never dies (except in your diseased brain). When talking with conservatives, talk about Jesus, Regan, the flat tax, fiscal responsibility, HRC, the deep state, the swamp, the troops, and the American battle cry for freedom. When talking with liberals, talk a lot about systemic racism, Gloria Steinem, goddess babble, male/white privilege, Sweden, single origin coffee, tarot cards, Marx, the patriarchy, astrology, and "burning the system to the ground." Talking about white feminism with white feminists, on the other hand, is forbidden because of white fragility and false equivalency. It's tricky. Also, don't forget to insert prefixes into normal words whenever possible to sound smarter than you actually are. Just like clean underwear and messy hair, unnecessary prefixes like *supra* and *meta* can be the difference between a monologue and a dialogue in the bedroom. Instead of talking about quiche, talk about meta-quiche. Instead of broaching the subject of the mold on your meta-quiche, try supra-mold. It makes no sense, but then again, neither does academic writing.

5. You tell Dikembe about the race card because he has no idea how fascinated white feminism is with Blackness because it sees false parallels between institutional racism and patriarchy while ignoring its own orientalist gaze and its racial and class privileges. Every time a white liberal gets lost in your world, lost in your hapa skin, lost in your racial hyphenation, there's an opportunity for evolution and self-interrogation. When talking

about god, always use the lowercase and say, *In a non Judeo-Christian way, I mean.* This is *really* important. Be sure to explain that Christianity is one of the major religions in Kenya (but don't mention Japan, that's a terrible example). With Black feminists, you don't need to explain anything because they already know more than you do and your game was up before you opened your stupid mouth, so you might as well pay the tab, thank them for their divinity, and walk the hell away because you're not ready.

6. Countercultural women of color know how to think for themselves, which means you're shit out of luck but also, you might have a dope conversation if you're humble enough. They'll call you out on your dead angles (and let you do the same) because they're genuinely invested in doing the work, most of it quietly, but they also know when to take a step back for their own sanity. After picking up broken men for ten years, they'll find any class, gender, or racial self-awareness refreshing in a post-Junot Diaz protagonist kinda way (just less machista). Since that's clearly not you, let the adults finish their conversation while you run outside to the jungle gym.

You ask Dikembe if he has any questions. When he says it's too much info, you shake your head and tell him he's a fucking idiot. *Okay*, you huff, *go buy fake glasses, preferably Guccis.* That's easy enough to spark a decent conversation with any human being. Black plastic frames are the best. The geekier, the better. Men that wear glasses appear deliberate and that's sexy. Your glasses will also create distance, which will put people at ease and might make someone consider drinking a coastal elite latte with someone as lazy, undisciplined, and clueless as you. Another thing: stylish glasses make you appear slightly unavailable, which you're not. Ugly is the new beautiful anyway, so he should be just fine with his Asian cheekbones and pretty Black skin. If by some insane twist of fate, the two of you end up at their (Wicker Park/ Logan Square/Edgewater/Lincoln Park) apartment and they have expressed unequivocal positive consent more than once for a kiss, slip a piece of fresh gum in your mouth (it's the least you can do) and take off your ugly Gucci knock-offs that make you look unjustifiably urbane. Fold the temples slowly into an X and slide them inside your jacket pocket like a checkbook. Now, get up and run as fast as you can through the front door, because you just used a fucking list to meet someone way above your pay grade. The world doesn't have time for your bullshit. Never did, homie.

(ANOTHER) ZEN (CLICHÉ)

1.

2.

3.

4.

---

1. cf. The Zen of Organic Lemons, 1.
2. cf. The Zen of Fake Designer Sunglasses, 93.
3. cf. The Zen of the Urban Asterisk, 113.
4. cf. The Zen of Zendaya in a Slow-Motion Rehab Music Video, 201.

EVERYDAY CORPORATE AMERICA

In the beginning, I used to ask myself the same question every day: Yuta, why play this game? Why spend your day in a little corporate cubicle like a cancer-study rat, writing your one-line emails to co-workers and ordering half your groceries from Amazon? Why pretend you like working in the dysfunctional world of IT? Why follow corporate protocol when you know it's one step away from professional robotics?

These questions are like canker sores I can't stop touching with the tip of my tongue. But I don't mind performing normalcy. My performance gives me strength. Sometimes, it feels like I'm a method actor for another version of me in another galaxy and sometimes I feel like the ensemble cast for my own biopic. There are even days when I forget I'm racing through the maze of market capitalism to retire by the age of thirty-nine. It has something to do with my 25-step ritual:

My 25-Step Ritual

1. Wake up early and reorder my 25-Step Ritual

2. Shower

3. ~~Take a shower~~ 3. Shave

4. ~~Shave~~ 4. Meditate

5. Iron one of twelve white button-downs given to me for Christmas as a gift from my parents, their attempt at grooming me for the starch-shirt world ten years ago when I graduated from Hope College with a nose piercing and a Prince tattoo and eyelash extensions

6. Eat some organic blueberries (if not, drink some "apple juice")

7. Pick up an almond mocha at Argus in my to-go cup and then take the #27 bus to work

8. Fight with feisty Chinese Grandmas on the #27 bus who expect to sit down when I get on first, loudly sipping my almond mocha and rejecting my Confucian programming

9. Fight with feisty Chinese Grandmas on the #27 bus who expect to sit down when I exit, which I oblige

10. Speedwalk up sixteen flights of stairs

11. Take the elevator to the 40th floor where I pretend I'm not thinking of a particular Robert Coover short story

13. Say good morning to all the CompSci rejects and economic jocks (i.e., coworkers) as I enter my office (i.e., cubicle with benefits)

14. Shuffle, bend, fold, and randomly mark paperwork without actually reading any of it

15. Look up baseball stats, Harry Styles FanFic erotica, laundromat addresses, and Google the word "lint" before checking my inbox for emails from Japanese politicians

16. Take a "vape break" (i.e., stand outside for ten minutes and stare into space)

17. Send business faxes to my otōsan, who gets really confused

18. Doodle on a notepad, masquerading my own list of Japanese snack foods as a list of office supplies

19. Eat vending machine snacks (the Frito-Lays are the best deal but have the least taste—a classic junk food conundrum)

20. Go to the bathroom and take care of my business, thinking about succubi, mud wrestlers, and Princess Peach cosplayers

21. Go back to the Rubik's Cube (aka my rat maze cubicle)

22. Shuffle and wrinkle more paperwork before faxing my list of Japanese snack foods to my otōsan with the

subject heading, "TOP SECRET," which always con-
fuses him

23. Make some phone calls, preferably to psychic
hotlines without time limits

24. Email coworkers about the stack of papers I haven't
read yet

25. Voilà, it's time for lunch already

Sure, this ritual gets old pretty quickly and, sure, I have my
professional ambitions like every other college-educated dotcom-
munist, but I also have other things to keep me sane.

For one thing, I create YouTube videos of female mud
wrestling with sad rock playing over it. There's nothing more
rewarding than watching angry white women slopping around
in a big pit of mud and taking out their rage against the patri-
archy to slowed-down Radiohead songs that apparently no one
watches.

Another thing, I wear knee-high stockings and SPANX
underneath my wool trousers. It's comforting and helps remind
me of my own complexity. Everyone here thinks I'm Yuta the
baseball fan, Yuta the sake fanatic, Yuta the former lieutenant,
Yuta the former Scrabble champion, and Yuta the Android
apostle. It might be the tight embrace of my lower body or the
secret knowledge that I'm making multimillionaire IT pur-
chases in biker shorts and silk hose but, tbh, it's just comfy. If
my co-workers only knew how contradictory and destabilized
gender performance is to me, how fluid my identities have always

been, and how much I keep them all at arm's length to protect the semantics of my own existence, they'd be shocked.

Beyond that, I like to drink cold miso broth. I know that might sound gross or kinky at first, but it's neither. Miso shiru is simply what happens to soybeans once they've lived a little. We're so used to pristine water that we forget that purity is not a color, it's a concept. Its color reflects its experiences the way wrinkles display age. It's the perfect amount of saltiness and umami and has been shown to protect against stomach cancer too. The problem is that my coworkers act like I'm bringing a Sterilized Vitamin Drink with me, (i.e., a big glass of pee). White people can be pretty racist, even the good ones, but their unconscious racism is a rabbit hole I refuse to jump down. So, I drink what I drink, ne? Sometimes I just pretend it's apple juice.

The problem with knocking back miso broth is that I know what it is but I also know what my colleagues think it is, so I'm incredibly self-conscious about it. *Man, this miso broth is bomb,* I'll declare, which always makes a couple coworkers raise their eyebrows. I think it has something to do with the fact that I always bring it in this big Crate and Barrel glass (Saran Wrap covering the top with a rubber band) and refuse to drink it with tofu cubes or wakame. My coworkers and I get along well enough, just the whole miso-in-a-glass thing that dampens the mood. Someone will be telling a funny story and the instant I bring it out, everyone just stops talking (or they pull out their phones). It's a little frustrating, to say the least. Occasionally, I even have to pretend to spill my miso (remember this trick). *Damn,* I'll shout robotically, *I guess I have to go buy some more miso from that Japanese restaurant across the street.* The hard part isn't the acting though. The hard part is that I have to drink cheapass miso afterwards that tastes like a million soybeans pooping into my mouth while the tofu and wakame gag me with every sip.

My passion project, however, is my lint art (no relation to Hannah Wilke's body of work). Sure, most people just throw away their dryer lint, but I actually create art out of it: I create multicolor landscapes out of your Jockey's. I've recreated the Tokyo Tower, made several world atlases, and constructed thousands of impressionistic landscapes from my girlfriends' underoos. I even sent Prime Minister Abe a portrait of Malcolm X from black and white tube socks. I never got a response back from him.

If you're wondering why I usually end up dating femme women instead of say fashion designers (which I have, by the way, and they wear nothing but black—it's terribly disappointing for my lint art), I'll tell you: femme women are better cuddlers and they have the most colorful laundry. That's why I always fall for mixed-race and BIPOC women in bright pastels, in part because they're completely aware of what it means to harness and celebrate vivid color in this white-washed world and I can't wait to do their laundry either. They don't have to know that I love them as much for who they are as I do for their vivid shirtdresses. Besides, I bring a lot of emotional intuition to a relationship. My love-making skills are on point. I'm really affectionate, I'm obsessed with romance manga, and I have an infectious joie de vivre that comes from knowing who I am and who I love. As we lie in bed and she holds my grease-soft hands, whispering jokes to each other in pillow talk, me kissing her shoulder until my lips melt into her skin, interlocking our fingers until our bodies are webbed with desire, her holding me tight with the driest and roughest fingertips I've ever known and kissing my torso and forehead until the pleasure burns inside me like a solar flare, I know in that moment that I'm safe, loved, and understood. I also know in the back of my mind that sometime in the next couple weeks, I'll spill wine on my shirt and say, *While I'm at it, why not throw some of your stuff in too, babe?*

My art has even become the topic of wine parties and chat rooms. *Did you see Yuta's lint mural of Dragonball-Z above the fireplace?* Women in A2 love men who understand them because cishet dudes don't have a clue. And hey, I'll do their laundry too if we fall in love. As for me, relationships give me the thing I want more than anything: dialectical infatuation, emotional evolution, a tennis match of trust and desire, a safe space for our contradictions, a triumph of human connectivity, and also a perfect palette for my lint projects to express a talent the Buddha gives only his worthiest and most hopeless visionaries.

THE MYTH OF THE MYTH OF THE MYTH

1. Meta-Symbolic Subtitle

The first thing fabulist narrative hero told me at site of magical realism in quaint northern Michigan town is that his mythical genealogy (classic Fairytale genre convention) is like a narrative diorama of a diorama (p. 21).

2. Alienating Subtitle

Once upon a French Vowel, you turned into a Goldfish qui parle français, forcing your mom to hire a translator before she delivered the fatal blow (p. 157).

3. Opaque Subtitle

You can call me Cryptic & Infuriating (pp. xx-xc).

4. Cryptic Subtitle

You can call me Electric Sky Church. Or not (p. 169).

SOLA'S ASTERISK

If destiny is not a fortune cookie, then it's a used book, something we read over and over again that passes from hand to hand and shelf to shelf, each reader leaving a trace of their life on the pages. Destiny is everywhere because it's an innate and immortal human tendency to look backwards at life. The Turks and the Greeks see destiny in lumpy brown coffee grinds, Jackson Square tarot readers measure it according to wallet size and time of day, Nostradamus searched for it in bowl of water, and palmists read the highways of unwashed fingers, fondling intersections, and back-alleys. Sad intellectuals and unknown poets search for it too, intoxicating their senses in musty bookstores and lofty lecture halls, percussive greasy spoons, and monastic libraries. It's precisely because destiny is everywhere that—pardon the truism—people obsess about it but never see it. This is why, even though Sola had at least eight different destinies she could have picked yesterday, ultimately, she was only aware of one of them at a time. In the end, our faithfulness to destiny is always based on the timeline we're living. If destiny is everywhere, though, then how can there only be *one* destiny? How can there be only *one* Sola? It's 2006 and no one knows the answer.

Yesterday

Sola drank her first cup of warm almond milk at her breakfast nook, gazing through her window at a large puddle on the sidewalk that looked like trouble. From her CD player, AIR's *Moon Safari* floated through her open window, drifting into the morning air: the opaque sunlight, the crystalline drizzle, and the temperamental spring sky. Chicago weather was notoriously schizophrenic. Sola watched the sky dance in the puddle's reflection: its metal liquid surface distorting the yellow tulips in the foreground and the oscillating cityscape of the Loop in the distance. Sola clicked the side of her mouth, like she'd just taken a picture, and then put on her jacket. She put on her sunglasses outside and walked in the direction of the Harold Washington Library, just as the rain stopped until she came to a six-stop intersection known unaffectionately by Chicagoans as The Clusterfuck.

Before her baby-blue sneaker hit the tarmac, Sola suddenly remembered her overdue library books. At Thursday night at 12 A.M. Central Standard Time, according to the Harold Washington Library Account Office, Sola's books became overdue.

Pause: the matchbox traffic on Lake Shore Drive came to a bizarre halt, their bright primary colors captured in urban meditation. The clouds froze in time in the plastered horizon, goose wings formed perfect V's in the catatonic sky, a patterned blue rubber ball stopped inches from the dirty fingernails of a boy in striped overalls with red balloon cheeks. The ripples on Lake Michigan became a field of delicate glass. A scurvy boy on Michigan Avenue lit his girlfriend's cigarette with a shiny new Zippo, the yellow paintbrush flame motionless in his hand.

Sola's untied shoe hovered in the air. As she wine-tasted the cause and effect of every choice in a manner of milliseconds, she didn't know, she couldn't know, that each street she chose would become a different destiny with a different (parallel) world. She wondered: what if god is just a role-playing game? A coherent narrative coined from a set of observed circumstances? What if my life is nothing but a divine lottery? What happens once I put my foot down? How flexible is my destiny? Can I reverse it? And will I be haunted by all the choices I didn't make afterwards?

Destiny #1: Right on Merchant Street
(The Steeple Chase)

Sola put her foot down and took a right on Merchant Street.

She passed three old men playing dominoes on an abandoned desk under an oak tree with burning, lava-red leaves framing their bodies, practically aspiring to radiance.

—Nikos, the first man exclaimed, puffing on his cigar, if you got that double 4, drop it.

—I'm stuck, Boli, the second man lamented, scratching his cap.

—You dumb Zorbas! You can't remember a damn thing! the third player shouted as he snapped his suspenders. He picked up his last domino and slammed it on the table like an OG in a '90s rap video.

—The double four! the man with the cap cried.

—The double four! the man with a cigar bellowed.

—Yup, how'you'like dat?

—Oh, *dammit,* Alexis! the man with the cigar moaned.

—Add'em up boys, add'em up, the man in suspenders sang victoriously.

Sola chuckled as she passed a magazine stand with college boys skimming cleavage shots, several Greek restaurants named after family members, a small French bakery with a royal blue fleur-de-lis on the open door, and a flower store, its black buckets on the sidewalk swelling with lilacs, blue bottoms, carnations, and cawing birds of paradise. Sola stared down the storefront of a rare book dealer that was never open and then passed a popular deli, its front windows crammed with Turkish delight, dolma, and baklava. She stopped when she saw a train of little pink bodies pirouetting in the dance studio window above. Her jaw tightened as she crossed the street and gave a hostile side-glance.

When Sola arrived at the Grecian Urn, one of her favorite cafés hidden from Zagatslaves and aspiring existentialists, she grabbed the door handle when she heard someone call out her name. She turned around and saw—to her horror—Antonio Plobada scurrying across the street like human vermin.

The short man with wide glasses, disheveled beard, stained sweatpants, fanny-pack, and bulging red eyes used to stalk Sola until one moonlit night she moved out of her apartment in secret and changed her phone number. Sola's throat became parched as she gripped the door. Antonio crab-stepped towards her. She turned the knob behind her back but it was locked. The Grecian Urn didn't open for another fifteen minutes.

—Hellooooo there, Sola.

Her eyes scanned the sidewalk for a El staircase or a police station globe or a good Samaritan before returning to the stumpy man reeking of stale coffee, fried food, and dried paint. His right hand shook uncontrollably at his side.

—How the folks? They doing good?

—Just dandy, she said, not knowing why she'd chosen that word.

—Glad to hear it.

—So, listen—

—And how's the new place? he asked, moving closer.

—Listen, I don't think we should—

—Wait, what's the rush, sweetie? he asked, only inches now from her.

—Yo, I gotta go.

—Sola, wait!

—You're supposed to leave me the fuck alone!

—Come'on, wait a sec—

Sola speedwalked down the sidewalk. Antonio followed. The next thing she knew, she was bolting down Merchant Street, Morrocan tote bag in hand, with the sketchy Antonio Plobada trailing her a block behind. She ran between kissing SUV's, imperial yellow taxis, and a group of Japanese tourists taking pictures of the Sears Tower.

In Antonio's mind: *And it looks like the lanky bi-racial hottie has a sizable lead on her Italian rival. Look at the ease with which she jumps over children playing on the sidewalk and hurdles over a yellow taxi like she's doing the triple-jump. Amazing! It looks like the Americans are still a dominant force in track and field, ladies and gentleman. But wait! It seems that Sola Matsumoto's competitor is closing the gap. Despite stubby legs and heavy fanny-pack, her Italian "friend" is making an impressive comeback. Antonio Plobada may not have technique, ladies and gentlemen, but he* sure *seems to have a heck of a lotta determination! This race is getting tight! He might even—oh! Antonio Plobada runs into a flower stand! Can you believe it? A* flower *stand, of all things! What a* terrible *disappointment! A* horrendous *setback!*

The sky became a Japanese fairytale of raining flowers: white mums, white pansies, white tulips, baby's breath, and pink and lavender hyacinths all spiraled through the air and blanketed the damp sidewalk where Antonio lay, stunned by his clumsy miracle.

Sola ran inside a Blue Line station and slid her Chicago Card frantically through the turnstile. Antonio screamed her name in the distance. Clusters of white rose heads stuck in his beard as he struggled to stand up, buried in a mass wedding of paired carnations. Sola ran upstairs onto the platform as an old Vietnamese man played his electric mandolin to an instrumental version of Alanis Morrisette's "Ironic." Sola slipped through the closing doors of the El and sat down, panting. Antonio waved his fist in the air like a manga villain tricked by misfortune.

He who will not be named was just slain by flowers, she thought to herself.

Destiny #2: Orbis (The False Prophet)

Sola put her foot down and stayed on Orbis Street.

She didn't want to waste more time, so she walked straight ahead, passing the window of an expensive gym with 30-something women dressed like the Spandex Army, their sweaty bodies floating on ellipticals, a strategically placed pizza kiosk with reggae music blaring out of the calzone counter, and a small chiropractor called Get Back to Where You Once Belonged. She passed Wong's Video Killed the Radio Star and a White Hen Pantry with an Illinois Lottery sign that read: *68 Million and growing. Will today be your lucky day?* She passed two white women in country club pastels, chatting in front of a tiny chocolatier while their Shi-Tzu's had sex like it was no big thing. Sola passed two boys with flawless skin, matching silver necklaces, and moussey haircuts holding hands as they window-shopped at a Korean bed and bath store. She passed a Vienna Beef stand where a Latino family was nibbling on hotdogs and French fries as a little girl watched her two brothers scarf down cheese fries with unblinking big brown eyes, her pigtails hovering in the air like handlebars, tied in glittery blue and red hair bands. Sola looked up at skyscrapers in the distance that looked like glorified plywood models dipped in broken glass. Little V-shaped formations flew heaven-bound towards the outer limits of the horizon as Sola crossed the street in the shadow of urban giants.

After Wacker, Lake, Randolph, Washington, and Van Buren, she arrived at the Harold Washington Library. Sola went inside and sat down in front of a vacant computer: Eight-five new messages in her inbox. 189 in the junk folder.

—God, I fucking hate Microsoft! she muttered to no one. Sola was the last person in her circle of friends without a smartphone, so looking up her email on a computer was still a thing for her. Mostly, she wanted to protect the element of surprise every time she opened up her email, but her relationship with Hotmail was making her rethink that decision. After blocking offers for unsecure credit cards, money-grubbing alma maters, shady business deals from wealthy princesses in Senegal who needed help investing their vast fortunes in American savings accounts, and instant access to webcams of Eastern European girls who were clearly immortal, Sola read an email by her mom, written in kanji she couldn't read anymore but could probably guess anyway. After cutting and pasting her mom's email into Google Translate, Sola read in confusion: *Has there been a knocked unconscious who is leaving a cornfield of the maker? Forgotten my camera name? How is the Tigger? These boxes of ballet shoes are what to the world? A samurai is calling, asking for your new address, but there are no names for the names. There are the things which names are not.*

Then she read an email from her younger brother, Taiga, who wanted to go out for Thai in Lakeview sometime later in the week and introduce Sola to one of his nerdy art friends, she was sure, who was probably creepy, stunted, and trying to start his own sex cult. The next email was for Free Tibet, which Sola subscribed to but never read. It was basically guilt in a newsletter.

The next real email was a long, desultory letter from her friend Sonnette, who'd been living in Burkina Faso for the past year and wrote these epic emails whenever she made it to the capital, retelling her adventures as a Peace Corps volunteer who was fighting to ban female genital mutilation, educate local communities about HIV transmission, and create solar-powered communities using NGO muscle. It was an alternate world Sola didn't really understand still knee-deep in college electives and city life. She could barely imagine living a life no one understood on the other side of the world. She almost didn't understand it herself. But every time she read one of Sonnette's emails, she understood how vastly different her life could have been if she hadn't taken a gap year traveling through Japan, Vietnam, Hong Kong, France, Spain, and Poland after high school and then another year in the middle of college to get her head straight after an abusive ex shattered her psyche like an anarchist swinging his bat at Wall Street. In every new update by her friend, Sola got lost in her own daydreams, contemplating how different her whole life could have been if she'd made different decisions, had her shit all figured out, and was as organized and efficient as Sonnette, whose emails seemed to float in cyberspace, rising up into the sky of Sola's imagination like an encomium of the human spirit, always warning her about the joys of free will and the plot twists of counterfactual love stories. Every image of her friend's life in West Africa seemed to burst in Sola's face like paint balls. Who knows what life choices Sola might have made if they had graduated from college at the same time? Who knows where she might be right now? Instead, Sola felt like a child collecting candy on the ground from her friend's smashed piñata, Sonnette's emails exploding with stories of bustling African markets, farmers tilling moribund fields, slender functionaries aboard mopeds speaking in fake French accents into their cell phones, elephants going on pilgrimage in the Savannah, claustrophobic bush taxis, and spikey Mossi palaces. She was Sola's free pass to the world.

When Sola was done reading, she clicked on the last unread email:

Sender: WristSlitter773.

She took a deep breath. She had a bad feeling about this:

my sweet little Solita

i'm lost i'm writing you because recently my gothnicity has started to scare even me i can't get my shit together and i feel paralyzed by a dark and terrible dread please help me i need you right now you are my only light in this dark, festering hole some call my mind time is running out and the industrial steel razor blades in my medicine cabinet are starting to sing their funky siren song i don't know how long i can resist my own doom

Desperately,
–L

PS: bring some gooshers when you stop by I'm all bones and bile from the melancholy and white guilt

Sola gulped hard. She hadn't talked to Linus in forever. She still hated him for his uncanny dramatic magnetism and she still felt guilty about breaking up with him two years ago in the middle of a heinous poetry slam at the Unicorn Café, just before she flew to Osaka in case she met any cute Japanese boys or decided never to come back. But she still cared for him. It was in her circuitry, man.

She had a feeling he was bluffing, but the wager was too high and Linus knew she wouldn't backhand his threat, even if she sensed a trap, because deep down Sola was more afraid of ignoring an opportunity to save someone than she was of wasting her own time trying. Besides, she kinda wanted to know how her non-binary, mascara-wearing-I-wish-I-was-Robert- Smith ex-boyfriend was doing. She left the library shaking her head. The day had been stolen from her.

Sola walked three more blocks to the Jackson El stop and then down the staircase, which reeked of piss, Doritos, and cigarette butts. She slid her Metrocard through the turnstile and walked to the platform. Depressed and defeated, she leaned over the platform and squinted. There was a faint, wane glow at the end of the tunnel. As the train lights became louder and more blinding, Sola wished she could freeze time and remain on the platform forever, safe from a world of mock suicides, crowded trains, and Gothic joysnipers.

Destiny #3: Right on Merchant with Books in Hand (A Light Breakfast)

Sola spun around and put her foot down on Orbis, turning back.

Truth is, she hated debt in every possible form, whether it was credit card debt, social debt (e.g., being forced to help a manipulative friend) or family debt (e.g., the guiltbombs her Japanese American mom dropped on her routinely). Sola felt like she had no choice but to go back to her apartment and fetch her overdue library books, so she ran up the staircase, skipped a step, and unlocked the door. She gathered her books, stacked in two perfect piles on the kitchen counter and stuffed them in her Moroccan midnight-blue and off-white tote (technically, Bedouin). Her hand was on the doorknob when the answering machine clicked on: *Hey, you've reached Sola, so leave a message. If this is Antonio Plobada, I don't know how you got my number but I'm moving to a Rainbow Family Commune, so leave me the fuck alone!*

Beep: *Hey Laso, it's . . . Linus.*

—Linus? she asked in disbelief.

Listen, about the email I sent you last week. I know you probably won't write me back and I just wanted to say thanks because that helped me realize that, um, that I have to do this myself. So, thanks for not babying me. That was, like, a big help. Love you!

Sola glared at her answering machine. —What the *hell* is he talking about? she wondered.

On the front lawn, Creuser, the landlord's beagle, was chewing on the obnoxious giant yellow tulips again. Sola squatted on the sidewalk to pet her. —You go right ahead, honey. They're ugly anyway. The mischievous dog wagged her tail. Sola got up and marched back to The Clusterfuck, taking a right on Merchant Street where three old Greek guys were playing dominoes on an abandoned desk in the shade.

—I quit, the man in suspenders yelled, —you guys are a bunch of rotten dolmas.

—Come on, I just took t'many dominoes, the second man grumbled, flicking his cigar.

—Yeah, try *four* dominoes too many! the third man shouted. He pulled off his pageboy cap, scratched his head, and put his cap back on.

—You guys don't mess around with your dominoes, do'ya? Sola said.

—Miss, the man in the cap said, all we got are naggy kids and domino cheaters.

Sola laughed.

—So, you a student? the man in suspenders asked.

She nodded.

—You got a fella? asked the man in the pageboy cap.

Sola shook her head, charmed by the old man's phraseology.

—Why the hell not? the man in suspenders asked.

She shrugged her shoulders. —Who knows? But honestly, it's okay. The last thing I need right now is some boy playing with my heart and demanding my attention.

The men burst out laughing.

Sola chatted for a few more minutes and then said goodbye, thinking about the last thing the man in suspenders had said: —You've got the whole world ahead of you. Your life isn't even ripe yet. Not like us old guys who drag our memories with us wherever we go.

Sola strolled down Merchant Street, passing the Demos Diner, The Stephenopolos Café, and a Tibetan Bookstore, Nag Champa incense blasting through multicolored prayer flags in the doorway. She saw a closed shop called Flower Power and a prohibitively overpriced art gallery selling acrylic paintings of anthropomorphic spoons. At the Grecian Urn, hidden from Zaggots and heliophobes, Sola opened the door and walked inside to the smell of hot olive oil, fried eggs, and freshly squeezed juice. She ordered orange juice and a mushroom-Gruyère omelet before looking outside the window and sighing. She sipped her orange juice, the sweet fleshy pulp swimming down her throat, when she saw Antonio Plobada scurrying across the street past the café, melting into the quiet morning air like a slasher villain.

Destiny# 4: Walking Down Kendra's Alley (Hang the DJ)

Sola put her foot down and took a left on Kendra's Alley.

She passed two reincarnated condominiums, an orientalist French restaurant called Indochine, an old Chinese theater playing "barely old" Hollywood movies and Bruce Lee classics, a barricaded adult bookstore that reeked of saw dust and disinfectant, and a tiny park filled with businesspeople in navy suits and power skirts eating sandwiches while nearby pigeons shuckled over breadcrumbs, bobbing their heads up and down.

She looked up at the Sears Tower, the skyline like an immense Botero cityscape, and then walked into a vinyl store called Jesus, Don't Cry. She handed her Moroccan tote to a pale employee in the requisite black slayer t-shirt and black beanie. He handed her a laminated #13. Sola walked around the aisles until she came to the electronic section and then picked up a used record in the S column. Intrigued by the chiaroscuro cover art, she asked Slayerboy if she could listen to a few songs when an overconfident 20-something Asian guy in a motorcycle jacket, ripped jeans, and barbed wire facial stubble grabbed her arm and said, —You don't wanna do that. That record blows.

—Well, I *like* Sasha and Digweed! she huffed.

—You can do better.

—I don't need your help.

—I'm not saying you do.

—And I don't need your indier-than-thou top-10 list either.

—Fair enough.

Sola squinted her eyes at him. —Look, aggressive guys annoy the *shit* outta me. They're pushy, easily bored, and predictably insensitive, and I'm the antithesis.

—Good word.

He stood there and stared at her in awkward silence.

—Okay, she said, can we get this over with? You're freaking me out.

He shook his head. —*Damn.*

As they bantered back and forth inside the store, Sola realized he was unjustifiably overconfident. She could practically smell his arrogance a mile away. He had that boring, predictable character defect (many American men had) of covering up his shallowness with sarcasm, and it was this less-than-perfect-performance-so-call-me-on-it-if-you-dare quality that she found unstable and grating. Intuitively, Sola resisted any hint of his formulaic charm, but she felt her body responding in a way that bothered her.

His real name was Haruto, aka DJ Hanshin, an overhyped DJ from Kobe who had a large following of high white ravers at his beck and call, which put Sola on her guard. She hated DJs: they were basically producers with good ears who knew nothing about music but everything about human sexuality. DJs were slutty demagogues, pandering to sexually repressed, catharsis-starving dancers who treated the dance floor like a therapy session. DJs were parasites, leaching off the creative life-force of starving musicians who had to bag groceries and shine shoes to pay for studio time. DJs were sellouts, making a living by spinning old vinyl to drunk college kids on moral siesta.

After an hour of talking shit to each other, Sola and Haruto went out for drinks at Liar's Club because foreplay. They talked and talked for hours, arguing the merits of Utah Saints, Loops and Tings, Digweed, Oakie, Gigi D'Agostino, Vienna House, Juno Reactor, Soft Dub, and Electropop. They agreed on nothing, both convinced they understood musicology better (though Sola was right more often). At the first conversation lull, Sola stood up to leave.

—Yo, where you going? he asked.

—I'm gonna pay the bill and get going, she said.

—Why?

—I've gotta study.

—You like to be in control, don't you?

—Says the Floor Nazi.

He chuckled. —What's the dealio?

—Try being a woman for a day.

—Tell you what. You can pay the bill if you come hear an album I'm mixing.

—Where's that exactly?

—In my loft.

—Not in a *million* years.

—See? Haruto said, you've got issues. I can see right through your city-girl façade.

Forty-five minutes later, Sola walked into Haruto's loft in Wicker Park when he threw his keys on the table and slammed the door behind her. She watched him strip off his black leather jacket and light a pre-roll, which she judged him for inside her head. He took a deep drag, staring across the room at Sola who avoided his gaze, turning instead to look in the window at a couple on the sidewalk down below, confiding in each other about something, an act of solidarity she craved suddenly.

And then in an instant, it happened: Haruto turned Sola around from the window and placed his lips passionately on hers. She opened her mouth, feeling his hot breath as their tongues swirled around in a carnal and fleshy dance that sent electric currents through their suggestive bodies that had been registering seismic tremors in silence for hours now. Haruto's hands slid down her sides, softly circling her hips and inner thighs. Sola crossed her legs. He lowered her on to the floor, opened her legs, pulled down her blue-striped tights, tore off her panties, and licked his way up her quivering thighs as Sola gave surprised groans spelling out her conflicting feelings of aversion and arousal. The emptiness burned between her legs.

When they were done, Haruto snored in bed with a smile carved into his cheeks, his tattooed arms resting Byronically on his chest. Sola walked to the Damen stop and took the El home. In front of her door, she searched for her Tokyo Tower keychain before shouldering her way through the door. In the kitchen, Sola pressed the playback button on her answering machine and walked into the bathroom and turned on the shower in a daze. Her skirt, tights, and torn underwear slid to the floor as she placed her t-shirt and cardigan gingerly on the toilet seat like they were a delicate flower arrangement. She climbed into the steamy shower, plopped down on the tiled floor, rested her head on her forearms, and closed her eyes as the hot water smashed into her head, exorcizing the demonology from her brain. From the kitchen, the answering machine jabbered on: —*I just wanted to say thanks I guess because that helped me realize that . . . that I have to do this myself. Thanks for not babying me. You helped me out more than anyone. Love you. Ba-bye.*

Sola couldn't hear a thing because she was looking through the bathroom window for something, for someone that wasn't there, for an alternative version of herself that had rejected Haruto's advances and gone to a café in River North instead to read Banana Yoshimoto short stories and eat an almond croissant for dinner. As she raised her forehead into the jet stream, she decided that DJs only knew how to manipulate the human body. That's all they were good for. She felt stupid for letting Haruto devour her for sport, his life unchanged by her pathologies of love and defection. She'd given away a tiny piece of herself and he'd added it to himself to become larger than he was. The emotional asymmetry ensnared itself into her every thought. Sola decided she would never fuck someone again who didn't hold her hand in bed.

Destiny #5: Left on Merchant (La vie en Rose)

Sola put her foot down and took a left on Merchant Street.

She passed a computer store advertising "The Greatest Desktops in the Tri-State Area" and an African crafts store with Mossi masks guarding the entrance and skinny wooden warriors standing in formation, reminding her of Sonnette's life in West Africa. Sola saw a crêperie, a laundromat with signs that read, *fresh paint, no touch,* and a whole block of nondescript bars with large screen TV's and Ludacris blaring from jukeboxes. She passed a going-out-of-business magazine stand, a cluster of loft apartments with rusty fire escapes and tiny grills on the balconies, and a pink Montessori school on the corner.

Sola stopped to tie her gym shoe again. As she held the two laces in her hand, she looked up and saw a shiny red ball bouncing into the arms of an ebullient boy in striped overalls, his cheeks flushed and jubilant. She smiled and made a clicking noise from the side of her mouth. She stood up and walked past a tiny boutique called Hoodie Rat. For some reason, today she opened the door and walked inside, not sure what she was looking for.

—Has it stopped raining? a voice asked behind the counter.

—The weather doesn't suck, Sola said, if that's what you mean.

—Thank god. A young woman dressed in a plaid jumper and panda hat stood up from behind the counter and wiped invisible dust from her jumper.

The saleswoman began folding sweaters on the sale table.

Sola looked around the boutique, yanking hoodies from racks that caught her eye to examine them closely, sometimes rubbing the back of her hand against the fabric. Eventually, she stopped in front of a stack of spring clothes and picked up a solitary pale-green hoodie with a #3 on the upper left chest. She picked it up, unzipped the front, and slipped it on. She walked over to the three-way mirror and swung from side to side admiring the soft cotton-Lycra texture and the '70s retro design.

—That hoodie's dope, the saleswoman said before resuming her folding.

—And this is my favorite number too, Sola said, pointing to the navy blue #3.

—Today must be your day.

—Must be.

Sola bought the hoodie and tried not to read into destiny too much, but she couldn't help appreciating the confluence of texture, color, and numerology smashed into one piece of clothing, and all for a hundred bucks! Clearly, she was meant to buy it, at least, that's what she told herself when she looked at her checking account balance four days later and moaned.

Out on the sidewalk, Sola was in consumer rapture as she crossed the street, nearly colliding with a hipster couple smoking cigarettes, their skinny arms wrapped around each other's waists. After flicking their cigarette butts on the sidewalk, (*Don't litter, you assholes*, Sola hissed down the block), the scurvy boy pulled out and lit his girlfriend's Camel Light with a shiny Zippo, its yellow paintbrush flame like a tiny cobra.

Sola passed a flower shop. The white roses and pink carnations looked like clones of impressionism, but the lilacs looked just like ballet shoes. She smelled her hands and grew pensive when suddenly, cathedral bells rang in the distance followed by a soft chorus of cars trumpeting their horns in celebration.

Destiny #6: Kendra's Alley with Books in Hand (The Blue Mirror)

Sola put her foot down and turned around.

Once, a devout Buddhist friend of hers who used to live in the apartment above her casually argued between sips of Pinot Noir on the back porch that debt was how humans steal from reality. In order to pay for a life they cannot afford, she said that they have to borrow from their future and steal their freedom from themselves. Ever since that conversation, Sola has overthought the meaning of debt for most of her adult life, so she walked back to her apartment, up the staircase, through the front door, and into the kitchen. Her answering machine was babbling: —*So, anyway, thanks for not babying me. That helped me probably more than anything. Love you. Ba-bye.*

—Who the hell was that? Sola wondered as she gathered her

overdue books, stuffed them in a "Midwest is Best" canvas tote, and locked the door. She ran down the stairs à la *Run Lola Run*. On the front lawn, Creuser was chomping on giant yellow tulips that formed parallel lines on the sidewalk. Sola blew the little dog a kiss. The dog wagged its tail. Sola stood up and walked to the intersection of Merchant and Orbis. She stepped onto the sidewalk and took a partial left on Kendra's Alley, passing a tiny falafel shack that smelled of garlic and lemon juice, a cluster of empty retrofitted condos, and a Moroccan café called Le Petit Fez. Sola passed two skaters grinding past a windowless adult bookstore with the words Taboo and XXX in big cinnamon-colored letters and a half-empty park with breadcrumbs scattered on the sidewalk like broken vows. At the next corner, Sola saw a Baby Gap window with miniature boots and small striped t-shirts that made her feel sadness for something she didn't even want.

Once she saw the John Hancock Building in the distance, which looked like the world's largest Lego, her blue gym shoes made soundless steps on the sidewalk as she walked into a tiny vinyl store called Vanilla Ice Must Die. She handed her vegan purse and crammed tote to one of the clerks and took a laminated 3, which brought a smile on her face. Sola paced through the aisles until she came to the Electronic section, browsing through Ibiza, Buddha Bar, and Hed Kandi compilations until an album with a striking chiaroscuro design caught her eye. Sola asked the saleswoman in the "Coldplay Sucks" t-shirt if she could preview the album, who placed the vinyl in a turntable and disappeared.

Sola listened for a few minutes, moving her head from side to side underneath large headphones that swallowed her dyed blond hair. The beats were seductive, but the melody was emaciated. Final verdict: catchy, but derivative.

—How was it? the clerk asked chromatically.

—Decent, but not revolutionary.

—Ain't that the truth about music today?

Sola handed her back the laminated 3 and retrieved her bags with both hands. —Bye, she said.

Sola walked down the street until she came to intersection connecting Orbis Street to Kendra's Alley. She passed a Russian restaurant with the faint smell of Chicken Kiev lingering in the threshold like the ghost of a cardiac victim, a small bookstore with posters of Maxine Hong Kingston and Chang-Rae Lee looking like graphic dictators for AAPI Month, and a sprawling billboard that read:

The Illinois Lottery
We Don't Play with Cash Money Giveaways!

A taxi honked at Sola as she walked through a red light. She gave him the finger. He honked again. A slight breeze rustled through her hair as she passed a liquor store called Ship of Fools (a Cubs game blaring on an old hand radio inside), an overpriced bed and bath store called WATER, and then stopped at a Vienna Beef stand. There was a squashed pile of greasy French fries on the sidewalk glistening in a coagulated puddle of ketchup. She made a clicking sound with her mouth before stepping over the smushed food and jogging up the steps of the Harold Washington library.

No one was at the check-in counter. Sola tapped her nails on the countertop and looked around, but only saw creepsters looking at internet porn in broad daylight and a few students reading the *New Yorker* and *I.D.* in the Primrose Study room, sneaking bites of granola bars and potato chips as they slouched. Sola looked through the library windows for a second and then looked up, where she saw a giant Chagall fresco in the middle of the library ceiling. Why had she never seen this before? It was hiding in plain sight, looking as if an interior decorator had stuffed Chagall's dreams into a plastic champagne bottle and then detonated it on the ceiling, every image, every stroke, bursting, dripping with swirling blue spaces, wavy green diasporas, and embracing stick figures. The icy ceiling with its gold clusters and shivering lovers reminded Sola of her ice-glazed bedroom window in January, the coldness of her sheets at night, and the quiet desperation of the clunky radiator in her overheated apartment in the spring. The ceiling mural was a frozen lake threatening to thaw on everyone. It was an explicit space of secret and private beauty, an artistic hallucination both dispelling and attracting her loneliness and heartbreak. She made another clicking sound with her mouth.

—Can I help you with something? a voice asked, appearing out of thin air.

Sola snapped out of her beatific vision and turned to the librarian, who had an asymmetrical bob and wore a brown turtleneck and English major glasses.

—Oh hi, Sola stammered, I need to turn these bags in. I mean, books. Sola opened her tote and stacked the overdue library books into three piles on the counter. In her mind, however, she was still stargazing at the ceiling, which felt like an ambient portrait of her own isolation.

—Here, Sola said, buttoning up her cardigan and walking away in a daze.

Destiny #7: Left on Merchant with Books in Hand
(The Recess Bell)

Sola spun around and turned back, running back to her apartment and up the staircase. Inside the kitchen, she gathered her books from the table, stuffed them in a paper grocery bag and closed the door. At the first major intersection, she took a left on Merchant where she passed a Korean Methodist church, a computer store advertising "The Greatest Desktops in the Tri-state Area," a cluster of overpriced cafes with olive-oil filled glass fish on square tables overcrowding the sidewalk, a brown Jewel Osco straight from the '60s, a smoky new-age bookstore wreaking of patchouli, Kitaro and taiko drums pounding in the background, a crafts store called Bead That As It May filled with awkward teenagers dipping their hands into jars of ceramic beads, a group of Hasidic Jews chatting in front a synagogue with large Hebrew words above the entrance, a crêperie called Ma Double Vie, and an old Laundromat with signs taped on the front door that said:

Fresh Paint.
No Touch.

As Sola bent down to tie her shoe again, she held the laces in her hand when she heard a recess bell ring followed by little feet trampling on a playground. She looked up to see kids in Catholic uniforms running to the proctor. Ever since she'd started ballet in 6th grade, Sola's life had been a continuous race against time. In middle school, she overworked herself, slept sporadically, and fumbled through dating (which her parents were relieved about). In high school, Sola went to Interlochen Arts Academy where she became anorexic, rebellious, sexually unsatisfied, and cynical about boys, which was easy to do in Northern Michigan. Her friends were mostly dancers who spent every waking hour practicing through shin splints, bleeding toes, sprained ankles, swollen heels, crash diets, and mental exhaustion, too busy imitating professional ballerinas to fully live their lives or develop their bodies. Her senior year, Sola changed majors, became a photography major, and enrolled in every photography class she could get her hands on where she gained five pounds, lost her virginity to a piano major named Miles, and walked around Northern Michigan with a camera slung around her shoulders like a Second Amendment fanatic.

It was at Northwestern that Sola discovered who she was by rejecting who she would never be. She would never be like her friend Sonnette, who had her whole life figured out at the age of sixteen, Excel spreadsheets and all. She would never speak nihongo fluently, even after years of Japanese school in middle school on the weekends and emails written in obscure kanji from her mom. She would never be André Kertész. She would never weigh ninety-seven pounds. To the explosive disappointment of her Japanese American mom, Sola became a fine arts major and then promptly stole her Canon 670 digital camera, the one with a telescopic wide-angle zoom lens that had been hiding in the basement. In time, Sola crushed on verbose nerds in her lit classes, especially the ones that did magical things with language she'd never thought of doing before, she took day trips to Andersonville to study inside bohemian cafés, and read graphic novels and Japanese short stories in translation obsessively. It was in college that she was forced to grow up. She had her first one-night stand, her first vodka blackout, her first psychedelic trip staring at burning cigarettes and melting faces on the beaches of Lake Michigan, her first rave in the West Loop, and her first abusive relationship with a boy named Daron Bradley Klines who faithfully loved her until the day he broke her left arm in three separate places when she arrived two hours late to his dorm with Marlboros in her pocket and whiskey on her breath. A woman's autonomy was a dangerous thing to a broken man.

Her loss of innocence had been painful. She loved college despite its tragedy. She loved children despite their blindness. But she'd always had issues seeing kids follow the rules of adulthood considering what a huge fucking mess it actually was. Kids should be running around in circles, playing tag (no touchbacks), the surprisingly violent Red Rover, HORSE, dodgeball, and Spies and Agents, a game that she was *always* picked to be the spy, a microaggression she didn't understand as a hapa kid because of how badass spies seemed to her. Kids should just ignore adults. Kids should do the opposite of whatever adults told them to do. Kids should be break-dancing in the middle of class, getting in trouble, kissing in the art closet, and making swans out of construction paper. That was their irreversible childhood destiny. Someone should tell them. Someone should have told her.

Sola stood up and entered a little boutique called Hoodie Rat, a sadness spreading through her body like an odorless nerve agent. She looked around the sale rack and sighed.

—Hey, how are you today? the saleswoman asked.

—I've been better, Sola said. You?

—Meh, the saleswoman said, removing her panda hat. They looked long and hard at each other. —Do I know you from somewhere?

—I was wondering the same thing, Sola said.

—Naperville Central?

—Interlochen.

—U of C?

—Northwestern.

—First Presbyterian Church on 97th street?

—Bahai'i temple in Wilmette.

—Nine Inch Nails at the Aragon?

—Yeah Yeah Yeahs at Logan Square Auditorium.

—Fetish night at China Club?

—House night at Shelter.

—Hmm.

—Wow.

—Okay, then.

Suddenly, cathedral bells rang in the distance. They both listened intently. Sola saw St. Catherine's Middle School where, as a girl in love with Madonna outfits, Q-Tip songs, and Beyoncé videos, she'd decided to become a professional dancer. She saw herself untying her ballet shoes and running after her friends during first recess, just as her childhood began mutating into adolescence.

When the bells finished ringing, Sola walked to the door.
—See ya'later.

—Have a good one, the saleswoman said, a note of sadness in her voice.

—Yeah, you too.

Sola closed the door, stepping on warm cigarette butts, and walked back home in the breezy afternoon drenched in bittersweet sunlight. The streets were redolent with old rain, wet earth, and sweaty ballet shoes.

Destiny #8: Orbis with Books in Hand
(Sunset Kodak)

Sola turned around and ran back to her apartment, up the staircase, and into the kitchen. She took a quick pit stop in the bathroom and stuffed her overdue library books into her blue and white sequined Bedouin tote from Morocco, drank a second cup of room-temperature chocolate almond milk, and then ran out the front door without locking it.

On Orbis, she noticed women in aerobic fatigues floating on air, a sterile coffee shop with plastic pastries, a shiny fire truck backing out of the double garage (FDC-27), and a rug store called Ali's Exotics. Sola walked three more blocks and passed two stuffy-looking white women in country club pastels giving air kisses to each other in front of a tiny chocolatier as their Shi-Tzu's struggled against their leashes. Sola passed an old Arab guy leaning on his cane and staring at lavender soaps, aromatherapy candles, and fluffy down pillows in the windows of an overpriced bed and bath store. She imagined him as a young WWII soldier, buying chocolate and postcards in Paris for his exhausted wife whom he had not seen for two years since their last spoiled kiss on Navy Pier.

Sola passed a Vienna Beef stand where a large Latino family blocked the sidewalk. Two brothers were fighting over a boat of French fries when the larger one yanked the boat from his younger brother as he was reaching for a French fry. They laughed and yelled at each other in weaponized teenage Spanglish while their little sister looked on with astonished brown eyes. Finally, the older brother gripped the cardboard boat while the younger one pulled as hard as he could until the cardboard boat split into pieces. French fries flew in every direction like shrapnel. Sola dodged them before they plopped on the sidewalk with a mute thud.

Two blocks away, she glided across the street, just as the light was turning, and entered the library. After taking two escalators up, she walked towards the circulation counter and waited. She tapped her nails on the countertop. But she only saw sketchy guys in sweatpants and food-stained t-shirts on the internet and a few college students reading today's *Trib*. Sola looked around the massive library, through the windows, and then up towards the ceiling when someone interrupted her.

—Ma'am, are you with the Yamamoto Senior Tour Group?

—Ma'am? Sola asked in horror, before turning around. This is when time stopped for the second time. The librarian was the most beautiful hapa boy she'd ever seen. Afrolatino, maybe Blasian or Japanese Brazilian? She couldn't decide, but he was definitely mixed-race like her. With his black button down rolled up to his elbows, pierced lip, gold and brown facial stubble, soft avocado-green eyes, mocha skin, and messy, skater boy hair, the tips dipped in honey, he looked like a daydream. Sola had expected a white, uppity librarian in oval reading glasses and cardigan covered in cat hair, not a moment of urban rapture.

—Um, she said.

—Okay, well that's a *start*, he said.

—Oh god, sorry. I get distracted by art.

—Where's the art?

She bit her lips. —I'm dropping these off.

He began scanning her books:

Snapshots of Tokyo: 1947-1997
Portraits of Blue

French Nudes
Zurich and the Hobby Horse
The Life of Cartier-Bresson
The Collected Letters of André Kertész
Naked Women, White Sky
Kitchen
The Second Sex
Lizard
NP
Nan and Violence
LaChapelle Hotel
Erotic Robotic

—So, are you a photographer? he asked, smiling with his eyes.

—Well, I take photographs, if that's what you mean.

—It's not, actually.

—Oh.

—Anyone can take pictures. But not everyone is a photographer.

—I'm having flashbacks of my analytical philosophy class, she said.

—God, sorry about that. Sorry you took such an awful class.

—Don't be. It was the only class I ever aced without studying.

—That says a lot about your work ethic, you know?

She couldn't figure out his tone, so she gave him a skeptical look.

—What I mean is, why photography and not, I dunno, graphic design?

Sola bit her lip again and thought long and hard about it. — Well, with art, you're creating something beautiful or theoretical that didn't exist before. Something that responds to our culture. Something that makes an argument about our world. But with photography, you're *capturing* the quanta of the fleeting world. The objects of photography don't have to be strange. It's the perspective, the arrangement, and the point of view that's special with great photography, not necessarily the images themselves.

—But I mean, what's the point?

She shrugged. —When you capture something beautiful, you prevent it from dying.

—But there's something to be said about embracing the cycle of life.

—Well, all things die, she said, that's the *point*. But with one snapshot, you can immortalize a fleeting moment forever.

—That's a bit heavy-handed, he laughed.

She smiled because she found his laugh strange and endearing. —Well, death is heavy-handed.

He nodded his head, smiling. —Yeah, I guess you're right. He scanned the next pile of books before looking at her again. —Can I ask you a question?

—Go for it, she said.

—Are life and art the same thing?

Sola bit her lips, thinking about his question. —Life is just unexamined art. Life is just art before the frame.

—Cool argument! I'll have to think about that tonight when I take a bath and cry myself to sleep.

Sola smiled, her hands resting on the cool marble desk while he typed something on the computer. —So, what's your name? she asked, surprised with her forwardness.

—Luca.

—Luka? she asked, as in, you live on the second floor?

—Yes, he said, and if you think I haven't heard that a *thousand* times, you're wrong.

Sola laughed into her hand, a bad Asian habit of hers. Or so her mom said.

Luca waved his hand at her in protest.

—I'm sorry, she said, laughing, I'm not trying to be a dick. Her laughter bounced off the hidden ceiling mural. The magazine flippers and internet creeps turned their heads towards Sola who was now in hysterics.

Luca shook his head. —Well, what the hell is *your* name? he asked laughing. —Lemme guess, Amélie Dutch Mimosa?

She covered her mouth with her hand again. —Sola, she whispered.

—*Sola?* he shouted incredulously. What the hell kinda name is that? Is that like Sula?

She squinted her eyes at him. —No, it's the fifth and sixth notes of the Solfeggio scale.

Luca glared at her. —Oh, well that really clears things up.

—Look, my dad named me Sola because I used to kick my mom's stomach when she sang Cole Porter.

—Uh huh. Whatever you say.

—And my mom agreed because Sola means "destiny" in Japanese.

—Also "sky," FYI.

—Wait, are you hafu?

—Yeah, Japanese and Brazilian, but my Japanese is fucking horrendous.

—At least you *speak* it, she said, my nihongo makes me sound like a kid.

He nodded, his eyes shimmering with intrigue. —So, how

does it feel to have two completely different meanings for your first name? And are you sure you're part Japanese? I'd never know it from looking at you.

She mad-dogged him. —Hey, not looking Asian (as much as that wounds me) is the name of the game for hapas.

—That's true, he sighed, but who names their kid "destiny?"

—Well, who names their kid after a song about child abuse?

—It's not *spelled* the same way.

—Whatever you say, Mr. I-live-upstairs-from-you.

He bared his teeth. —You see this?

—Your crooked teeth?

—Hey! Well, this is the sound of me snarling at you.

—At least you're open with your aggression.

—Girl, I don't even know you and I wanna bite your fingers. Sola gave him a dirty look. —I don't date cannibals.

—From the look of things, you don't date. Period.

Sola felt a surge of anger in her that almost felt like joy. He was right, she hadn't dated in a long time, not since she'd broken up with Linus to spend a semester in Japan where she mostly read manga in English, took night shots of Tokyo, Osaka, and Kyoto, and played MarioKart with her Japanese friends, only making out now and then with Japanese boys she met at parties, who were usually prettier than she was and had better hair too. Now, she wanted to look away, but she couldn't. ~~Luka~~ Luca smiled at her with his soft and adorable green eyes, the irises burning with gold filaments. She was transfixed. She was sprung. She felt like Luca had teleported into her timeline somehow and now she wanted to know everything about him. She wanted to know what his favorite cafés and neighborhoods and El lines and boutiques and Japanese restaurants in Chicago were. She wanted to know the stories of his life because every mixed-race person was a story. She wanted things she had no right to want from him. She wanted to smell his body in the morning, fall asleep with him on her futon, binge on *Naruto* and the Kieślowski trilogy, and go out for sushi dates at Ora. She wanted him to fuck her on the balcony in the canopy of night and have picnics with her in Edgewater on the weekends, even though she would never admit any of these passing thoughts. She wasn't crazy.

A big part of Sola wanted to confess everything she'd been feeling, just so she could hear the words reverberate off the roof of her mouth and understand how it felt to confess the truth with her own lips, shaped by her tongue, committing herself to the prophecy of her own syntax, to the artifice of her own language, and to the vibration of her own phonemes. Part of Sola wanted to walk away right now before she got hurt. Before the stories she'd created inside her head about Luca were torn apart and razed to the ground by the bulldozers of reality as they had so many times in adulthood. Sola forgot how she ended up at the Harold Washington library, telling Luca things she'd never written in her Tumblr account or admitted to her closest college friends unless she got good and drunk on free sake. She forgot about her little studio. She forgot the feeling that had been ghosting her all day of having lived, having lost, and having imagined a series of alternate worlds that weren't hers to claim or remember. Now, all her memories were out of focus, her life narrated in the whisper of other fading destinies. Sola had no idea what was going to happen. She only knew the singular experience of being alive right now. The true and honest feeling of stumbling on serendipity for the first time in years.

Several hours later once the library closed, they walked down the front staircase together. The sun burned low and fierce as if the foundry of clouds had poured molten rays of sunlight into a giant circle of rage and desire in the Chicago skyline. When they reached the sidewalk, Sola stopped. —Hold on a sec, she said, I wanna remember this.

Luca looked dumfounded.

Sola placed a finger on his lips. Their warm softness lit a fuse inside her body that would burn silently until the first time they made love. She looked at him standing on the library steps, his beautiful light-brown face framed in ethereal cobwebs of sunlight, and then she made a clicking sound with the side of her mouth.

—Okay, I'm ready now, she said with a nod.

Luca smiled at her, a blaze of joy and intrigue smoldering in his eyes, just for her. As they walked down State Street holding hands and chatting for the first time, their hearts throbbed in a perfect harmony of fear and joy and longing.

This is not where the story ends, just where we say goodbye.

FOUR HAPPY SONGS FOR THE SKATEBOARD

1.
She did an Ollie Impossible in the parking lot, right on Zen Street
(p. 59).

2.
He did a Judo Air right over the moon and into the Milky Way
(p. 616).

3.
On the half-pipe, she did a 720 Gazelle Flip and then a double
Lemon Conspiracy (p. 1).

4.
Dude, that Flip Trick isn't gonna cut it if your opponent pulls off a
Dolphin Murder Astral Projection Flip (p. 177).

ENTRANCE EXAM TO MY HEART

0. Sum Game

For the record, I'm not a cockblocker. I resent that term too because it makes it seem like I'm the one getting in way of all the fun, but fun isn't a natural right, it has to be earned. I refuse to compromise my standards for anyone, even myself. It must be the mixed Asian in me. That's why every Michigander that goes on a first date with me has to fill out a questionnaire and take a short exam. I admit, at forty-seven pages, it might be overkill. But I know I'm worth it and the right man will too. He *has* to. That's question #207: *Do you think I'm worth it? Using the Toulmin method, please construct a perfect rhetorical argument proving what my intellectual, emotional, social, and cultural worth is to you.* The rest of my First Date Exam is organized like this:

1. To Check or to Not Check (the Box)

The first section is a background check. I ask for his Social Security number so I can check his credit and debt history, the names and phone numbers of his last three employers in the Detroit area (I mean ex's), his place of birth, highest level of education, alternative names used in any collection agency avoidance scams, and favorite NFL team (it's Lions or bust). I also ask for a complete set of fingerprints to conduct a 1-959A multiphasic FBI background and investigation search. I had no idea how many terrorists, white nationalists, and incels were trying to get laid before they died until I added this search to the first section.

2. Perv Personality Tests

The second section is a modified Briggs-Meyers personality test. I refuse to date INTPs, USMCs, and NERDs. What can I say? I know what I like. The last part of this section is a homemade Rorschach test that I made with some of my daughter's finger paints I found in the attic after one spring clean. Men who see pornographic images in picture #3—a purple dot—are eliminated immediately. No pervs in my Japanese boudoir.

3. What's Your Sign, Dude?

The third section is the astrological, religious, shamanistic, and spiritual compatibility test. I ask for the exact time of his birth as well as his moon and ascendant signs, his Chinese astrology sign, Native spirit animal, and religious or "spiritual" affiliation. In general, I don't like dating Buddhists (which eliminates a lot of Japanese guys sadly) because they're obsessed with silence and they're too morally relative with everything. I need a loud man who knows when he's wrong. I also avoid Evangelical Christians, however, because they're too cut and dry when it comes to my own body. Again, I need a man who knows when he's wrong. Taoists and Rastafarians also get the boot. Come on, those aren't religions. Religions aren't supposed to be fun and games (and those have to be earned anyways). If your idea of a religion is sleeping with white girls in your co-ed dorm, devouring the snack cabinet, sitting on your ass all day, or singing "Redemption Song" at a Novi Karaoke bar, I can't imagine what your idea of a girlfriend is. Next!

4. Split My Infinitive (if You Dare)

The fourth section is a grammar test with a large fill-in-the-blank component. It's sort of like Mad Libs for prospective grammatology lovers. If you can't distinguish between a noun, a modal verb, and a predicate in English, you can't write me a good love note. I *refuse* to date a guy who doesn't know how to conjugate either. It's a pet peeve of mine, just like orientalism. In one exam, a white guy wrote "I heart you." Hel*lo*. That's a subject pronoun, a transliterated graphic signifier, and a direct object. Where's the dang verb, Mr. Action?

5. What's a Four-Letter Word for Ciao besides Ciao?

The fifth and final section has two parts. The first part is a crossword puzzle I made on my old Macintosh. The trick is that the crossword puzzle doesn't actually work. The clues don't make sense and the answers don't fit. If the guy is smart enough, he will give up and jump right to the second part, which is a large maze. I give the applicant, I mean, prospective dating partner, two minutes from the time he tells me he's giving up on the crossword to complete the maze. As the instructions explain clearly: *my heart waits for you on the other side of this maze called* "contingent destiny." *Will you find me in two minutes? Or will you give up like all the other grillmasters who pretend to be men, causing traffic jams on I-94 as they barrel down the highway in the winter in their huge S.U.V.'s, getting lispy-redneck-drunk on beer with monosyllabic names as they watch stupid rivalry football games on ESPN in yuppie bars in Corktown or the Old West Side or Heritage Hill or Old Mission that serve nothing but gourmet cheeseburgers, blunt wine, and artisanal French fries with stinky cheese and truffle oil while groups of verbose, grammatology-obsessed mixed-race women sit around at nearby tables dying for an ironic token of affection, a feline glance, a knowing smirk, a subtle but inscrutable wink, another free chardonnay* (this wine is too oaky, *I'd complain to the waitress, just to assert my own free will), another free young coconut drink I never asked for, another surprising conjunction thrown in the air, a piece of flung popcorn hurled at 45's face on the TV screen, a flippant remark about* Counterfactual Love Quizzes & Other Failed Exams, *my experimental short story collection I carry with me everywhere I go like a little red book (published by Nōh & Me Press in 2021, but who's keeping track?), a flirty glance spoken to no one, a correct pluperfect conjugation, or a scrap of Latin for Dummies scrawled on a bar napkin like* Quod tibi signum? *and* Mus in labyrinthum sum. *Jesus,* anything *with some heart or intelligence or passion. Are you just another pathetic, language hating meathead who likes to break things with your fists when you can't think of the right word, or are you the right man for this conjugation of love? Will you cross this terrible chasm that separates me from you and hold me in your marbled biceps until our skin becomes glued together like a piece of plastic burning in the microwave? Or will you stay in this 2-minute maze forever like a missing sock, clinging to my sports bra? Will you—Oops, times' up, buddy.*

6. Mus in Labyrinthum

None of my prospective boyfriends have managed to make it past the maze part. It's one big trick, I admit, but then again, so is dating. It's better that men understand how much work a relationship is before they try to rip off my jeans or steal my Nico midrise briefs while I'm sleeping to sell to rich pervs on eBay or make outlandish murals out of my dryer lint. Some of my girlfriends say I'm being too demanding and too unrealistic. They point out that I haven't had a second date in the state of Michigan for seven years as evidence that my system is flawed, but I don't buy that. Not one bit. I think my dating status proves that *mankind* is a failure, and frankly, that's not my problem. I'll just wait until they catch up or . . .

HE DROVE/SHE WATCHED/THE END

1. While she looked out the window, he watched migration season in the tumescent sky and felt the dull pain of every abandoned Midwestern town he passed (p. 203).

2. While he drove through the heartland listening to Kind of Blue on the radio, she looked through the window and wondered about what it would be like to go backwards in time and regain something she'd lost inside herself (p. 35).

3. While she looked out the window, he listened to his favorite NPR show, "Forty Sad Songs for Your Pet Frog" on the FM radio and chainsmoked Lucky Spirits (p. 43).

4. While his Prius stalled at the intersection, she wondered how differently her life would change, depending on which street and which direction her otōsan drove, each contingent destiny flitting through her mind (p. 113).

FRENCH VOWELS THAT MAKE YOU LOOK LIKE GOLDFISH

1. Traître

As long as I've known my son, he's had a thing for French. This obsession has driven my white husband insane, but now our son won't speak to us in English. It's gotten so bad that after four months of nagging and fighting in two different languages, we've had to hire a French interpreter. We don't know what he's saying otherwise. Charlie doesn't care. He says, *Fine, let the boy speak surrender monkey. See if* I *care?* But I'm his mom and caring is literally my job.

2. Monsieur Je-Sais-Tout

In junior high, when all the other kids were studying Japanese or Spanish, Shigeru wanted to learn French. I told him no one spoke French anymore and he said:

—Well, the French do.

—But you're not in *France*, dear.

—Mom, we're not in *England* either.

—I *know* that Mr. Smartypants, but *English* is America's language, I asserted. And Jesus's too.

He didn't like the Jesus comment. Shigeru thought Jesus spoke French, claimed the Son of Man had a soft spot for fancy French vowels that make you look like goldfish. Maybe that's my fault. When he was a boy, I didn't teach him Japanese because I

thought I was protecting him. I also told him God spoke every-
one's language, but I said that Jesus *preferred* speaking English
because it was practically universal. Shigeru ignored me for a
whole week. He's sensitive like that.

3. Gymnopédie No. 1

His senior year at Clare High School, Shigeru drifted away.
He took advanced French classes at Mid-Michigan Community
College. He stopped listening to rap music on the radio and
began singing along to Glee, Les Misérables, K-Pop, and Erik
Satie on his iPhone. It's catchy music, gotta say. Without rap
or football Saturdays, the house was quieter than an aban-
doned church. Cleaner too. But then Shigeru started wearing
tight black jeans everywhere. He started smoking these musky
cigarettes called Gauloises on the rooftop when he thought
we were sleeping. He wore scarves, even in the summertime.
He started reading highfalutin books about Habermas, the
joys of Beaujolais, and living in Europe on a shoestring. But
he wasn't getting in fights at school, he was getting straight
A's, and he hadn't impregnated a girl down the block, so I
never complained (even if I wished he'd join a judo team or
something). Charlie watched all of this with a hawkish eye. I
stopped him from breaking Shigeru's heart by threatening to
"accidentally" wash his white t-shirts with my pink scrubs and
make nothing but kale smoothies for dinner for a whole month.
I worried, though, how alone Shigeru might feel as one of the
only mixed-race kids at school. I worried that his sadness might
be festering inside him. I worried that he might already have
left Michigan inside his soul.

4. Le Bain mortel

The day Shigeru disappeared was the worst day of my life. It was more painful to me than when he passed through my birth canal (because there was at least joy and relief then). That day, an ER doctor talked to me like I was an idiot and a migraine started gnawing at the electrical cords behind my eyeballs and I came home and burned the hell out of the meatloaf in a failed bid of multitasking, and I just couldn't take it anymore, so I disappeared in the bathtub. I love my family. I love my boys. But I needed some time to myself that day, so I retreated into the bathroom to let Calgon take me away, and that's when I lost my grip on my husband. It was just one single moment, but that was all it took. That's all it ever takes with men to lose your life. Without me, this family would collapse. The first thing Charlie did when he heard me splashing in the tub was march into Shigeru's room and started viciously attacking him like a police canine apprehending a criminal. At least, that's what Shigeru's interpreter told me in his thick, almost incomprehensible accent. As the bubbles slowly evaporated in my bath, leaving the water gray and dismal like a polluted river, I tried to make out what they were saying, but the door was too thick. By leaning my head against the door, I managed to hear Shigeru say: *I don't want a Philistine for a father.* And the last thing Charlie said was: *And I don't want no French traitor for a son either. So there!* Of course, Charlie thought he'd had the last word and he did. In English.

5. L'Enfer et le canadien

After that, my family went to complete and absolute hell (and I don't mean Shigeru's two-month obsession with Dante either). It all started with French and ended with the fishbowl. Speaking

French became my son's protest against President Bush's smirk, against our all-American Christian family, against Freedom Fry-eating Republicans in Congress, and against every gun-toting small town in Michigan. It drove my white husband insane that we were forced to pay a French translator to understand our own son.

—Chiyo, *listen* to me, Charlie had said, enough is enough.

—What do you mean? I'd asked. —You don't get to decide when enough is enough because you've already given up!

—Well, I ain't gonna pay for some *Canadian* to translate my goddamn *son* anymore. It's fucking ri*dic*ulous.

—You don't have a choice, Charlie.

—Sure, I do. I'm choosing not to *pay* that stupid son-of-a-bitch.

—Jean-Luc is very nice.

—He's an idiot.

—No, he's not, honey. He's just Canadian.

—The Canadians are fucking idiots.

—Just because they're not American doesn't mean they're idiots. Even I can see how narrow-minded that is.

—You sound just like him, you know that? And frankly, I've got no problem not understanding Shigeru. In fact, I think it's better that way.

—Charlie, we've been through this.

—I know and I still say: if Shigeru wants to speak *French*, then he should *move* to fucking Gay Pair-ree. There was no irony in my husband's voice.

—He's seventeen.

—Well, that's a perfect time to move.

—He's a minor.

—Then we'll ship him off.

—That will cost *a lot* more than paying Jean-Luc.

—Fuck Jean-Luc. What kind of name is that? Why does he have *two* first names?

—I don't know, but your plan doesn't make sense.

—It makes a *hell* of a lot more sense than paying some frou frou French Canadian to translate my own son, whose native language, in case you've forgotten, is *ENGLISH*, the language of the constitution, the magnificent mitten, and Jesus Christ our Lord and Savior.

—Don't you raise your voice at me, I said, pointing my finger, —you want PINK UNDERWEAR again?

—*Noooooooo*, please, he whimpered.

I shook my head and started putting plates into the dishwasher because it was the only thing I could do. Sometimes, I was a terrible Christian. Sometimes, I wish I'd stayed a Shintoist.

6. La Sonnette

The doorbell rings. Charlie sighs and rolls his eyes.

—I'll get it, I say.

—Damn *right* you will, he mumbles, I don't want nothing to do with that Maple Leaf.

I open the door. —Bonjour Madame Heeks, ça va? Jean-Luc asks, kissing me on both cheeks. He is dressed in white jeans, loafers, and a blue Lacoste polo with a cream sweater tied around his shoulders. He looks fancy like always and smells like a resort on the French Riviera.

—Hi, Jean-Luc, I say, I'm fine. Please come in.

—Tank you.

—Shigeru! I yell up the stairs, please come down. We have a visitor.

I lead Jean-Luc into the kitchen. —Jean-Luc, do you want some lemonade?

—Uh, yes pulease. Zat would be great.

—One lemonade coming right up. Charlie, will you call Shigeru?

—No way, Chiyo. He'll come down when he's goddamn *ready* to.

I pour the lemonade into a glass with thick orange contour lines forming a half circle where your fingers are supposed to go. I pull the scoop out of the freezer and tinkle ice into the glass like a one-trick triangle player. The ice cubes chime the same note. I hand Jean-Luc his lemonade and then walk to the living room again.

—Shigeru Joseph *Hicks*! I yell, —this is the *last* time. You hear me?

Shigeru's door opens dramatically, the doorjamb vibrating like a didgeridoo. Shigeru marches down the stairs and inside the kitchen and sits down, all pouty and pretty. When he sees Jean-Luc, his smile is wider than the great state of Michigan and I know what I see.

7. Voie à sens unique

I open up the utility drawer, pull out a notepad, and sit down. Flipping to page forty-seven in my "Questions for Jean-Luc," I turn from Charlie to Shigeru. Then, I give Jean-Luc a nod.

—Okay, I say, let's begin. Jean-Luc, first off, please ask Shigeru where my car keys are.

Jean-Luc nods and repeats the question in French.

—Ses clés? Shigeru asks, bah, shais pas.

—He doesn't know, Jean-Luc says.

—Like *hell* he doesn't know, Charlie shouts.

—Okay, Jean-Luc, then tell him I don't believe him. Last week, I discovered a large *dent* in the driver's side door.

Jean-Luc translates my sentence.

—Mais, c'est de la foutaise! Shigeru shouts. C'est pas moi qui a cabossé cette espèce de merde.

—He said he didn't put zee dent zair.

—Goddamn it! Stop *lying*! Charlie says, who *else* could have put it there?

—Mais, de quoi est-ce qu'il parle? Shigeru asks.

—He says, what ahhh yoo towking abo—

—You know *damn* well what we're talking about! Charlie shouts again.

—Charlie, I say. Calm. Down.

—This is stupid, Chiyo. He knows everything we're saying.

—But we don't what *he's* saying.

—He's a fucking *teen*ager, Charlie says. We're not *supposed* to.

—C'est minable, Shigeru says, mon papa est un trou de cul et ma mère sait rien de rien.

—What did he say? I ask.

—He's talking about me again, Charlie says, right in front of my face.

—He says uh, well, zat me-stair Heeks is uh, note uh nice . . . and zat you . . . don't . . . un-dare-stand heem.

—Well, how the hell can we? Charlie screams. —Our son's a goddamn surrender monkey!

—Charlie, I say, you're not helping.

—Il est fasciste, mon père, Shigeru hisses.

—What? I ask.

—He called me a Nazi, Chiyo.

—Non, Jean Luc says, actually—

—Oui, Shigeru says, nodding emphatically.

—You little fucker, Charlie says. I oughta bop you right in the kisser.

—Charlie! I yell.

—Enough's enough, Chiyo!

—C'est vrai, Shigeru says.

—Okay people, I say. This is not helping one bit. *Forget* the car!

—Chiyo, no.

—Cette famille est naze, Shigeru says, looking sideways and exhaling dramatically through his lips as if he were smoking an invisible cigarette.

—Going on, people, I say, going on. I clear my throat. — Okay, Jean-Luc, please ask Shigeru if he's heard from colleges. He hasn't told me a thing and it's almost *April.* We're getting worried.

—I don't give a rat's ass, Charlie blurts out.

—Well, *I'm* getting worried, I say, and worrying's my job.

Jean-Luc repeats the question to Shigeru in French.

—Putain, ça? J'y vais jamais. Jamais de la vie!

—Uh, Jean-Luc says, he does not uh know.

—That's not what he said, Charlie says, scrunching up his nose.

—How do *you* know? I ask.

—I don't speak surrender monkey, but I can tell the goddamn *difference* between *I don't know* and *no way,* or whatever the hell Mr. Butter Croissant over there said.

Jean-Luc raises his eyebrows, wondering if my husband has said something racist. Shigeru pats him on the shoulder gently.

—Jean-Luc, I implore, is that what Shigeru said?

—Bah . . .

—Mais dis-lui, Shigeru says, je m'en *fous*!

—Madame Heeks, uh, he's not go-een to ooh-knee.

—What? I ask. He had a *perfect* verbal score on his SAT!

—See? Charlie says. Surrender monkey.

—That's unacceptable! I cry. I don't care if he goes to college in *Paris,* but he's *going* to college.

—Non, Shigeru says, jamais de la vie.

Jean-Luc pauses, turns to me and hesitates. —He says—

—I *know* what he said! I yell, and he's *going* to college whether he likes it or not.

—That's the spirit, Chiyo!

—Non, non, et non! Shigeru screams.

8. Le Coup

The next thing I know, my karate hand is a flat weapon, slicing the air with great and mysterious speed. I regret what I did. That's the truth. I regret the strength and the desperation of that moment. I regret the way I lost control of that situation, especially when everyone else was doing whatever they wanted. I have always regretted my actions, in fact, since my hand made contact with Shigeru's cheek, leaving a stinging red outline of India on his beautiful pale face, but I can't reverse what happened in the kitchen. I slap Shigeru with such shocking wrath that I knock him out of his chair like Ralph Macchio in Karate Kid (II?). Shigeru's tight black jeans are sprawled out on the kitchen linoleum, covering patterns of square-shaped flowers dulled by years of baseball cleats and later French wingtips. Jean-Luc looks up, terrified. Charlie is incredulous. But Shigeru, my little baby Shigeru, his eyes broken and glassy from months of protests and mistranslations, he staggers to his feet and grabs Jean-Luc's glass of lemonade and hurls it against the wall. Then he turns to me, his face wrinkled and adorable like an angry Shar-Pei, and shouts: —I *hate* you!

—Works both ways, Charlie mutters.

—I'm moving to France, Shigeru continues.

—As long as you go to college, I say, I don't care if you move to Patagonia!

—And Jean-Luc is coming with me.

—Shigeru, I say, let's talk about this.

—Jean-Luc loves me. And I love him.

9. Le Sol collant

And that's when Charlie's mouth falls to the ground like a broken coo-coo clock. Shigeru grabs Jean-Luc's hand and marches upstairs to his bedroom. Ten minutes later, he marches back down the staircase and through the front door with two Gucci suitcases I've never seen before and his favorite attaché briefcase, Jean-Luc carrying his I-heart-Alsace-Lorraine duffle bag in one hand and Shigeru's Goldfish bowl in the other—the orange fish making fancy, French vowels with their mouths as the water sloshes back and forth. The front door shuts with a single click and then the house is insanely quiet, pulsating with emptiness. Charlie walks over to the front door and locks it, shaking his head. I pull out the broom and start sweeping the broken glass into a pile as the lemonade streaks the wall in sugary vertical lines. I try to spot-clean the mess, applying a little pressure to the sponge, but the floor is sticky in all the places that Shigeru still hates me.

READER DESTINIES

After coming to a complex intersection (aka clusterfuck) in the middle of page, sentence, & paragraph, you (the reader) must choose one of the following streets because life:

1. SECRET CODES AVENUE (p. 35): An estranged hapa woman reunites with her Japanese American father for the first time in fifteen years.

2. 10 KOANS DRIVE (p. 59): A Zen monk meditates on stage for thirty days straight until the audience finally starts clapping with one hand.

3. EVERYDAY CORPORATE AMERICA STREET (p. 103): A Japanese American IT worker demonstrates the differences between 建前 (tatemae or "public self") and 本音 (honne or "inner self") in his job.

4. VIDEO GAME AVENUE (p. 317): An American otaku becomes obsessed with "Animal Crossing" and locks himself inside a bathroom stall of the Art Institute of Chicago. He vows to remain there until his island gets a five-star rating and he has the gold watering can.

ELECTRIC SKY CHURCH

I. 新宿は午前4時、シカゴは午後1時
(Shinjuku at 4 am, Chicago at 1 pm)

一。

At four in the morning, it was one of the only illuminated windows in all of Shinjuku. When Keiko had insomnia on the weekends, she'd take a long, hot bath in the hotel bathtub and scrub her legs until the water was cold and dark like a forgotten cup of hojicha. She'd walk around her room naked, smoke her vape pen, and gaze at Tokyo like an urban fangirl. Sometimes, she examined the stretch marks that had formed contour lines around her thighs like tiny nacreous canals in reflection. Other times, she sat on the windowsill, her body both warm and shivering, her moisturized legs smooth and luminous to the touch like the inside of a seashell. As she drank Midori Sours and chilled, rehydrating later with a glass of coconut water, she'd take another puff and study the electric diorama of Tokyo until she fell asleep leaning against the window.

二.

Keiko was born and raised in Tokyo. She knew Shinjuku, Ebisu, Roppongi, and Ginza better than her own neighborhood. Her otōchan owned a flower store in Asakusa. On her eighteenth birthday she'd eaten fugu and applied to law school in secret. On her twenty-first birthday, she fucked her French Professor in a Love Hotel overlooking the Sumida River, just to destroy every familiar object in her life. She never looked back. Now, she owned a condo in Ueno with a hand-me-down futon and a closet full of knee-high dominatrix boots she'd never worn outside and oversized sweatshirts that intentionally looked like artifacts of ex-boyfriends to ward off repeat offenders. On the weekends, she stayed in hotels to luxuriate in anonymity, to feel the brunt of her loneliness and the weight of her sadness. These tiny joys slit her numbness like bad paper cuts. From hotel windows, she could examine the frenetic world she was a silent victim of. Instead of looking for a husband in college or filling her void with a screaming family or settling for a sexless marriage, Keiko stayed single so her thoughts would always be her own, even if she chose not to have any.

After winning a series of high-profile cases prosecuting corporate malfeasance (which she'd been encouraged to drop repeatedly by male colleagues), Keiko made partner, but became trapped inside her office with the framed JD degree from Kyodai and a large desktop Buddha. Because her colleagues didn't know her, they counted the days until she got pregnant and disappeared. She'd rather snort rat poison than follow someone else's script, so let them wait forever. Inside her swanky hotel room, Keiko ate croquets and ebi frai. She listened to Mazzy Star, Dream Pop, and J-pop all night long like she used to in college. She watched the blurry taillights of early-morning traffic on the street below as airplanes floated high above like futuristic beetles and red fruit watercolors detonated in slow motion in the healing sky. The clouds filled with the pulp of the color palette and the city found its breath again.

囚 ·

Soon, Keiko would go back home to Ueno and feed Pizzicato, her three-year-old Tabby. She'd water her succulents, trim her bonsai, prepare hamachi onigiri and tsukemono for her weekly obento boxes, and vacuum her futon. But inside this Shinjuku hotel, she could be a witness of the city's clockwork. She admired the graphic design of its public spaces. She read the animated billboards, accidental semaphores, kaleidoscopic buildings, and pulsing communication towers. She cupped her hands and whispered something through the glass. She had no idea if her words traveled far. Keiko didn't care. Tokyo was the closest thing she had to a lover, the only companion she needed in her life, and the one city where every flashing light was a love song for the darkness and a protest for the dreamers.

II. Watching the Future, Listening to the Past

1.

After mom got remarried to a white architect, my twin brother and I moved to Wacker Drive to live in the future. For Yoshi and me, the honeycombed Marina Towers were a time warp to another dimension. After passing them every weekend for years, it was surreal to live in a Wilco album cover.

2.

Sometimes, when we had the whole place to ourselves, Yoshi and I sat on the windowsills in the living room and gazed at the cityscape of Chicago, hypnotized by the altitude and the majesty. At night, the skyscraper lights pulsated. I told Yoshi the lights were semaphores signaling to invisible trains in the sky. Yoshi said it was Morse code sent to us from Japan. I told Yoshi that if we broke the code, we could ride the sky train together. He said deal. I said I'll take you before the world explodes. I said it's the least I can do.

3.

Other times when we got bored, we watched the drawbridges opening for passing barges that bellowed their horns into the crisp air like metallic beluga wales. Yoshi said different boats blew their horns in different keys. He said if you recorded every horn song over a month and then played them into a continuous track, you got a song. He said just jazz standards though. After I thought about it all week, I decided that jazz must be the language of Chicago's architecture. Maybe, every neighborhood is a work of spatial improvisation. Maybe, every El stop is its own soundtrack. Maybe, every street is a measure. Maybe, every building is a musical note.

4.

We stood there for hours, looking down at the streaks of wet brake lights, waiting for the next solo. When mom came home, our ears were pressed hard against the damp windows like usagimimi listening to the gossip of the city.

PICK ONE STORY

4. You will search Ann Arbor for the perfect Thai restaurant. You will not find it until you drive to Ypsi by accident looking for an Asian supermarket that may or may not exist (p. 207).

   3. Blue is the last color you see with your naked eyes before you start wearing your knock-off Guccis around Ann Arbor religiously (p. 65 & 93).

      2. You drive from the Loop to Ann Arbor, listening to anime soundtracks, Taylor Swift, NPR, and calming podcasts because the world almost feels normal on the road, at least until you put your mask on and take a deep breath at the next gas station (p. 43).

         1. Naw, fuck this pick-one-story bullshit. I'm ready to end it all right now (p. 200).

SEMI-PERMEABLE MEMBRANE

You shouldn't be here, but inside your head, you've already escaped, that's what you tell the other inmates, but they just snicker like they've heard that before, so you tell the concrete wall that the cops arrested the wrong girl and you just happened to be at the same party, a little fucked up but basically in control, dancing to Common in the living room while your two best friends made out with the Brezinsky twins from Saginaw who love no one, not even themselves, but you're no gangbanger, you don't even know how to shoot a gun, you don't trust them because guns make efficient divorces, they kidnapped your papa and made a Buddhist lunatic out of your okāsan, in fact, if the police did their fucking research, they'd know you abhor guns and the idiots who use them to feel in control against the criminal world in their own heads, if they'd done their fucking job, they'd know that you *created* a club at Cass Tech called S.A.F.E. (Students Against Firearms Everywhere) for your papa, you've got forty-three members, including a secretary and a treasurer who always puts his milk money into the club safe, but rookie cops earn their stripes by knocking innocent people of color to the ground because we're the low-hanging fruit in a busted-up Eden, all they saw was the gun in your hands and a bullet hole in someone's car, they assumed you were as brain-dead as they are because they like their rules and their hierarchies and their qualified immunity and their one-way violence and their pretexts for dominating communities of color and they don't like nuance (except when they're on trial for shooting another Black kid), but this indisputable fact doesn't mean shit in your orange jumper now, they didn't know (they didn't care) that you actually yanked the gun out of Esteban's hand, they didn't care (they didn't know) that he arrived at the party just to pistol-whip a skinny scrapper in a Tigers cap (just another white kid trying to get his street creds), they didn't notice (they didn't understand) that there were multiple fingerprints on the barrel, they didn't understand (they didn't notice) that they'd scared away the witness testimony the instant they bumrushed the house like cable detectives, fuck, they didn't even do a ballistics test or corroborate Esteban's alibi or try to figure out the rest of the sawed-off serial number on the gun using probabilistic number theory, they didn't figure out that the gun belonged to Esteban's uncle, they didn't do their job so now you have to, all the cops saw at the party was you in the living room of another house party in another police occupied neighborhood, all they saw was you, the trouble child with a minor juvie record, the mixed-race, second-generation, hapa girl with a so-called attitude problem, a staggeringly high GPA, and a rap sheet of misdemeanors involving petty theft because you got caught stealing brown bananas, sushi rice, discount nori, and week-old tortillas for your fam, but it was the optics more than anything, they found you holding someone else's gun by the safety like you were afraid of getting contaminated by male violence, which you were, but when they saw the gun, they freaked the fuck out, they screamed at you like you were a threat to their existence, the rage pulsing in their eyes, like they were thinking, how dare you have my power, how dare you threaten my life the way I threaten you and yours every day, the poisonous irony of that moment of power inversion almost killed you on several levels, so you gingerly placed the gun on the floor in slow motion and then they tackled you, slamming your head against the floor and punching your kidneys and shouting into your ears not to resist even though you were just bawling to your ancestors for help, begging for intervention, scared of this fucking world that always celebrates your trauma and defends your atomization, you were whimpering into the grain of the hardwood floor, invoking your dead Peruvian papa to save you, praying to your Japanese mom to protect you, picturing your soul as it left your body and floated down the street and hopped on an inter-city bus, that's when the cops dragged you into the police cruiser and threw you against the window while your frenemies and part-time friends took their little videos on their phones from the safety of the sidewalk, posting your arrest on Snapchat but never advocating for you, not even subtweeting your injustice, they just left you to your fate, pretending an old hashtag could save another brown girl, that moment was real enough to take away the flame in your eyes and the fire in your heart, which was sometimes the only fuel you could afford in your old working-class neighborhood in the D where failure was a giant dome covering the sky, where moving up in the world could be misconstrued as class betrayal, as you lie in jail now waiting in your catpiss-scented cell to be arraigned, you imagine yourself passing through the thick window glass like the ghost of parallel lives, on the other side of the street you see all the free people idling in their office windows, drinking instant coffee with the push of a button, flirting by the copy machine, overdoing their laughter as they stare at their phones all alone, you see gorgeous Black women walking their toy dogs in front of the Wayne County Juvenile

Detention Facility, chatting to each other and vaping, waiting for their Lyfts in the crisp autumn chill like Empire divas, you see a Latino running around the block in a red, white, and royal blue jogging suit and matching headband, you see white yuppies in busy sweaters and curlicue scarves, bouncing on the sidewalk like fresh tennis balls as gold, burgundy and pewter leaves fall down from invisible trees that have no attachment to the world, but you do, and the sky shanks you every time you think about life on the other side of this window, you see your spirit running through traffic to the shelter of the darkest alley, continuing to the faded part of Detroit, the exquisite sky stabbing you in the heart every time you look through plexiglass while your soul travels to Esteban's house where your destiny was overwritten by racial profiling, gender performativity, and police protocol, you see the yanked police tape slithering into the sewer gutter, last night's signatures of sunflower shells, cherry pits, and blunt stains on the cracked sidewalk, you see the ghosts of every person you (thought you) knew last night, hovering around your little body, whispering to the illuminated space where you've astral projected to, this is when you sing along to the chapel organ inside your head for the funeral of your life, you see yourself as a series of spectral bodies, potential and real, counterfactual and imagined, replaying every decision you made last night but also every decision you were too fucking scared to make, you see every possible choice, every possible consequence, flickering side by side in metaphysical counterpoint, your whole life played out on the existential keyboard, you see that your escape from prison is a low-key shout-out to Nabokov because you're nerdy like that, magically teleporting you back to the moment before you fell from grace in this country of embedded racism and violence, back when there were so many different versions of yourself as a hapa girl, like being an ambitious teenager who thought she could change the world, like becoming a civil rights lawyer and deconstructing the racist prison industrial complex you're now a victim of, like being a bright mixed-race girl who wanted to get her PhD in race and ethnicity studies because she understood racial hyphenation, social injustice, racial erasure, and racial illegibility better than anyone in her family, like being an exotified person of color who was always mediating the cultural conflict of the American binary, which included being a Latina and an Asian who was too light-skinned for people of color and too ethnic for white spaces, there was once a time when you tried so hard to fall in love with this fucked-up world that kept on hating you for being alive, for stealing the electricity from the Detroit suburbs and bringing it back to your family like a punk Prometheus, and now you're here, stuck and sentenced to live all your other lives in a feverish dream world of the damned and the dying.

COUNTERFACTUAL LOVE STORIES
& OTHER EXPERIMENTS

GRATITUDE

I'd like to express my deepest love, appreciation, admiration, and respect to the following people:

LB, who is the love of my life and the source of everything that is beautiful and redeemable inside me. I wouldn't be here without you, Baby Moonshine, humoring me when I talked obsessively about this short story collection to you forever, supporting me when I was a poor grad student, encouraging me never to give up even when it hurt so much to continue and it felt like the whole writing world was sacando cachita. You always reminded me of who I was when I forgot and loved me despite my obsessions, even when I didn't deserve it. In so many ways, this book is as much yours as it's mine. After hundreds of rejections from agents, indie presses, and literary journals, this victory is ours. I would never be here without you. I love you more than anything in this world. Te amo, mariquita con todo mi corazón. Te festejo y yo festejo mi amor re-profundo y interminable para vos, ahora y siempre. I carry my love for you deep inside me. I scream my love for you to all the dead stars because they cannot look away and their songs cannot hurt us when we are together.

My **kazoku**, who has loved me when no one else would. Obāchan, Mom, and Chad, who believed in me and supported every artistic calling of mine when no one else would. We've traveled through so many emotional parabolas together but the one constant refuge in our lives has always been our ability to accept and love each other wherever we were in our lives. I couldn't have made it here without you three. I love you all so much. お祖母さんがどこにいても、 僕を誇りに思ったことを願っています。 お祖母さんの精神はこの小説のすべてのページにあります。 愛しています。 ひどく恋しい。A mi familia peruana, te amo muchíssimo. Vos sos la red de apoyo, el amor dinámico, la solidez, el pueblo, la alegría, la calma, y la verdedera comunidad que he deseado desde mi infancia. Soy re hincha de ustedes. Somos todos parientes consanguíneos. Son mi corazón.

Tons of love, respect, and appreciation for my insightful, smart, and gracious mentors at **Portland State University**, Nathalie Nadeau-Wright, who was my first creative writing mentor (and also the first person in my life to give me a chance to become a fiction writer when I was down on my luck—something I will never forget). Big hug to AB Paulson whose wicked sense of humor and openness to my experimental style made me feel right at home in Portland. Also, huge shout-out to my gifted classmates, friends, and fellow writers Kevin Friedman, Nancy Chevalier, and Leah Sims, whose suggestions, support, insight, and love have nurtured me and this manuscript in more ways than I can express properly.

Tons of love, respect, and appreciation for my smart, insightful, and gracious mentors, Valerie Sayers, Frances Sherwood, Steve Tomasula, and William O'Rourke, my mentors and friends at **Notre Dame** who gave me the gift of being part of an MFA program when I was about to give up. You all supported me and taught me so much about mastering, challenging, and also defying the rules of storytelling and I'm a better writer and artist because of it. Additional songs of praise and love to Valerie for getting me to care about my own characters and see them as living, breathing people. Lastly, huge shout out to my talented MFA cohort whose talent, observations, and insight made such a huge difference in my own evolution as a writer, especially Renée D'Aoust, Beth "Bee" Couture, Angela Mi Young Hur, Shero Sheikh, Lily Hoang, Tim Chilcote, Tom Miller, Brenna Casey, and Jared Haley.

Huge shout out to my smart, insightful, and gracious mentors at **USC,** including Aimee Bender, Viet Thanh Nguyen, TC Boyle, Percival Everett, Duncan Williams, and Bill Handley. Double shout out and extra hug to Aimee for her sustained mentorship, friendship, narrative insight, humanity, and emotional support (thank you for welcoming me into your storytelling world with your beautiful twins). Also, songs of praise, and an endless well of love and gratitude to my talented and generous cohort, Bryan Hurt, Amy Meyerson, Bonnie Nadzam, Chris Muniz, Anthony Abboreno, Lisa Locascio, Emily Fridlund, Heather Dundas, Michael Busk, Chris Santiago, and Alexis Landau, all of whom encouraged me in different ways to write in my own voice, language, and identity. You have all inspired me in so many ways to never give up on my own career by doing amazing things in yours that I celebrate wherever I am.

An obnoxious and loud shout out to my **writer** and **scholar** friends who I've met and needed along the way in this winding path of mine: Emily Saso, Joy Huang, Molly Pascal, Niki Gjoni,

Gabe Hudson, Beth Nguyen, Grace Lee, Jamie Ford, Lawrence Coates, Susan Ramsey, Peter Ho Davies, Karen Tei Yamashita, Matt Bell, Jolie Sheffer, Julie Buntin, J.E. Burton, Ryan Ridge, Ross Wilcox, Sequoia Nagamatsu, Alina Stefanescu, Siân Griffiths, Jenny Bhatt, Dave Griffith, Tara Betts, Robert Olen Butler, Jim Shephard, Michael Martone, Tara Stillions Whitehead, Heidi Durrow, Elise Blackwell, Lance Olsen, Chigozie Obioma, Matthew Lebowitz, Lisa Ko, Hasanthika Sirisena, Allen Gee, Raluca Albu, Karen Hattrup, Emma Sloley, Lorinda Toledo, Carlos Pintado, Matthew Salesses, Ali Eteraz, Rebecca Schiff, Jamel Brinkley, Gauraa Shekhar, and Lisa Hickey, for all supporting my dream and believing in me for all these years, even when I felt like giving up on writing altogether and joining a monastery à la Leonard Cohen.

The many smart, generous, and insightful editors with the sharpest eyes and the biggest hearts at *Witness, Columbia Journal, Quarter After Eight, M.E.L.U.S., BlazeVox, Arts & Letters,* and *Vol. 1 Brooklyn,* who gave these stories their first home and an audience, with a special shout out to Lorinda Toledo, Victoria Rucinski, Steve Coughlin, Jolie Sheffer & Gary Totten, Geoffrey Gatza, Allen Gee, Laura Newbern, and Tobias Carroll.

A huge and eternal thank you to the readers and editors at Noemi Press, with a huge shout out to Sarah Gzemski, Carmen Giménez-Smith, John Darcy, and Elia Chaves for all of their help with this manuscript. Thank you everyone at Noemi for taking a chance with these experimental stories in an era where number crunching and pandering to the white gaze is still normative in publishing. I'm full of love and gratitude for you all in ways I can never adequately express.

Last but not least, thank you dear reader for making me an author. I love you from the bottom of my heart.

ACKNOWLEDGMENTS

Stories from this collection were first published in various forms in the following journals:

"Conspiracy of Lemons" in *Witness*

"Kothar Shinka" in *Quarter After Eight*

"Everyday Corporate America" in *BlazeVox*

"Ten Zen Koans Translated from Japanese, Mandarin, Wu, Vietnamese, Thai, Fujian, Korean, Tibetan, Hakka, Javanese, Mizo, Nepal-Bhasa, Khasi, Buryat, Malay, Paiwan, Burmese, Ryukyuan, and Okinawan by Jackson Bliss, PhD" in *Multiethnic Literature of the United States Journal*

"Secret Codes & Oppressive Histories" in *Multiethnic Literature of the United States Journal*

"French Vowels that Make You Look Like Goldfish" in *Vol.1 Brooklyn*

"Living in the Future" in *Arts & Letters*

"Semi-Permeable Membrane" in the *Columbia Journal*